# A LONG RIDE BACK

My successful return to triathlon through a network of great friends.

**Steven Crenfeldt**

MBS Press (Mind Body Spirit)
A division of Pick-a-WooWoo Publishers

MBS Press (Mind Body Spirit)
A division of Pick-a-WooWoo Publishers
Nannup, Western Australia 6275

**Copyright © 2012**

The moral right of Steven Crenfeldt to be identified as the Author; and Leonie Paine as Cover Designer, of the work has been asserted by them in accordance with the Copyright, Designs and Patents Act 1988. All rights reserved. No part of this book may be used or reproduced, stored in a retrieval system, or transmitted in any form, or by any means electronic, mechanical, recording, photocopying, or in any manner whatsoever without permission in writing from the publisher, except for the inclusion of brief quotations in a review.

**National Library of Australia Cataloguing-in-Publication entry**
Author: Crenfeldt, Steven, 1976-
Title: A long ride back: my successful return to triathlon, through a network of great friends /
by Steven Crenfeldt
Edition: 1st ed.
ISBN: 9781921883279 (pbk.)
Subjects: Crenfeldt, Steven, 1976-
Accident victims--Australia--Biography.
Athletes--Australia--Biography.
Dewey Number:    796.4257092

**Publishing Details**
Published in Australia – MBS Press (Mind Body Spirit)
(A division of Pick-A-Woo Woo Publishers)

**Printed & Channel Distribution in US/UK/Canada/Aus**
Printed through Lightning Source (USA/UK/AUS)
**Available via:**

**United States**
Ingram Book Company; Amazon.com; Baker & Taylor and others
**Canada**
Chapters Indigo; Amazon Canada and others
**United Kingdom**
Amazon.com; Bertrams; Book Depository Ltd; Gardners; Mallory International and others
**Australia**
DA Information Services; The Nile; Emporium Books Online; James Bennet (Australian Libraries) Dennis Jones and Associates; and others

www.mbspress.com
The author can be contacted through the publisher

For My Family

Life is like riding a bicycle.
In order to keep your balance,
you must keep moving.

Albert Einstein

# Testimonials

The capacity for physical recovery is remarkable with the scars a mark of the trauma and the subsequent journey made possible when you add in the elusive mental strength. "Because I Can" could be "Because We Can" as that mental strength was drawn from an amazing collection of individuals focusing their energy to facilitate healing. Mateship is alive and kicking and worth thinking about on a daily basis.

*Prof. Fiona Wood FRACS AM*

*Winthrop Professor, BIRU, School of Surgery, UWA*
*Chair, The McComb Research Foundation*

If you're in sport for long enough, tragedies disrupt your life. As they say, there's only two types of cyclists: those who've crashed and those who are about to crash! But it's not just biking, I've had melanoma kill friends (RIP David Baxter, Jane Carney), as well as road accidents claim champions (David Morris to name but one).

Then there are those who are lucky enough to escape with their lives, but are left with challenges far more difficult than any sport can provide. Steve faced his own personal Everest for months in hospital, with horrific injuries that turn your stomach to read about. His courage to overcome them and return to the sport he loves is a testament to his courage and the support his whole team was able to provide. Ironman is such a lofty ambition - to finish is to have taken the preparation to its logical conclusion. But traversing the journey is the main game. Steve's story shows that the journey to Ironman WA (or equivalent), is just an analogy for life. To succeed is to love the journey, not just celebrate at the finish line.

*Mitchell Anderson*

*Ironman Champion, MBBS, Raconteur*

# Table of Contents

i. Foreword ................................................................. ix
ii. Introduction ............................................................ x
1. The Day It All Went Wrong ................................... 1
2. Because I Can! ............................................................ 9
3. Mind Games ............................................................... 17
4. Royal Perth Hospital – Intensive Care Unit .......... 27
5. Royal Perth Hospital – Major Trauma Ward ....... 35
6. Visiting Hours Are Between 8:00 a.m. and 8:00 p.m. ....... 49
7. Ironmen Don't Cry – Yeah Right! .......................... 57
8. Bedpans And Pee Bottles ......................................... 61
9. Shenton Park Rehabilitation Campus – Part 1 ..... 65
10. The Great Escape ..................................................... 75
11. Shenton Park Rehabilitation Campus – Part 2 ..... 81
12. Home – Finally! ........................................................ 93
13. The Land Of The Long White Cloud .................... 121
14. Back In The Saddle .................................................. 127
15. Solitary Confinement .............................................. 133
16. The Magic Of Thinking Big ................................... 139
17. The Starter's Gun ..................................................... 147
18. Party Time! ............................................................... 153

| | | |
|---|---|---|
| 19. | Reality Bites! | 157 |
| 20. | Round 3 | 161 |
| 21. | Not A One Hit Wonder | 165 |
| 22. | Negative Gearing | 179 |
| 23. | Mental And Physical Traction | 183 |
| 24. | Going Through The Motions | 187 |
| 25. | The Positivity Chapter - Eventually | 195 |
| 26. | 3 Years On | 201 |
| 27. | It's All About You! | 211 |
| 28. | Dear Diary... | 217 |
| 29. | Thanking The Cool Kids! | 221 |
| 30. | The Fab Four And Other Rock Stars | 223 |
| 31. | Further Acknowledgements | 231 |
| 32. | What Now? | 235 |

# Foreword

I was speaking to Steve on the Monday night prior to his accident and he was saying all the right things that a Coach wants to hear – feeling strong on the bike and itching to get out on the morning ride to hurt his training partners. His running was coming along nicely and his swimming (his Achilles heel) was even improving as well. Ironman Western Australia was around 3 months away. I got off the phone and told my wife that it looked like Steve was going to get his goal time at the Ironman. I went to bed a content Coach.

Tuesday morning came and the phone rang. One of his training companions was upset; telling me that there had been an accident and Steve was hurt, and hurt bad. He had gone under a truck and it was not good. They would be flying him to Royal Perth Hospital.

Later that day I went to see Steve in hospital before his first of many operations. He had nearly lost his leg and would take years to even be able to do anything normal again with it. Through the haze of drugs he was on to dull the pain, his one question he wanted his Coach to answer was 'Will I be right to race the Ironman?'

As a Coach and friend, how do you tell someone that they will be lucky to walk again let alone do an Ironman in 3 months; yet keep their hopes up for the years of rehabilitation that will be needed for an injury like this?

This is the story of Steve Crenfeldt, an average triathlete who loves the sport and embodies all that is triathlon. Never give up; setbacks are for getting over, even if they are big; and live to fight another day.

*Ross Pedlow*

# Introduction

On 14 October 2008, while training for Ironman Western Australia, I was on a group ride with a bunch of fellow athletes from Busselton, WA. I clipped the wheel of the bike in front of me and crashed, ending up in front of a truck, which was coming along behind us.

This is my story of what happened and how I got back doing the sport I love. The months in hospital, followed by rehabilitation and physiotherapy, as I tried to get close to where I once was or maybe a little better, in a perfect world. I was not chasing glory or even out to compete. Just simply trying to get to a position where I could swim, ride and run again and hopefully string it all together for a few triathlons.

It's about being average at a sport that I enjoyed and quite content with that. But when you suddenly become below average, getting back to where you once were is very, very hard work. There are highs and lows, good times and bad times, with a few tears along the way. So if you want to achieve something big or small, but aren't sure whether or not you can, then you might relate to this story.

But the most remarkable thing about my journey was not what I have gone through or what I have accomplished afterwards. It is that it was done without the presence of my family around me, something that is usually available to other people who have found themselves in a similar situation. Whilst I knew my family was only a phone call away and I was always in their thoughts, I feel the real acknowledgment has to go to the wonderful network of friends that made me a part of their own family and gathered around me from the time of the accident and continue to do so today. Without this support, the outcome of this journey would have been very different.

Competitors wait for the start of Ironman Western Australia, in 2007.
*Photo Credit – Belinda Higgins*

# 1

# The Day It All Went Wrong

*Life is a succession of lessons, which must be lived
to be understood.*
*Ralph Waldo Emerson*

The truck skidded for less than ten metres, but used my body like a snowplough as it came to a stop. The first thing I remember doing was wiggling my toes. Max, Michael, Steve and Alex were soon beside me, telling me I was fine, I'd be okay, the ambulance was on its way and I'd soon be at the hospital. Inside their minds however, was another story. Would I make it? How much blood had I lost? Where is the ambulance? Luckily though, I never sensed their urgency or their distress.

Tuesday 14 October 2008 was the day that changed my life forever. Affected as well, of course, were the lives of those around me, along with my friends and family who were soon to find out what had happened. The scheduled triathlon training ride we were on went from a solid session with every rider putting in the hard work, to an abrupt stop. The four cyclists I had been riding with were left wondering whether I was dead or alive. Max Higgins, Michael Bray, Steve Anstee, Alex Douglas, and myself had been in a group of about 10-12 riders out for the usual Tuesday ride. 2 hours hard, according to the program from my Coach Ross Pedlow and with these four in the group, it was hard and fast!

We had set out as a larger group of men and women at 5:30 a.m. and headed out of town on the usual weekday training course. I thought back to the words Ross had spoken to me less than 24 hours ago. 'Go out there tomorrow and smash it. Keep riding strong like you have been and go hard'. About 3 kilometres into the ride,

# A Long Ride Back

I pulled out and accelerated past the group. I knew that the majority of the riders would have followed me and kept up quite easily. I could work well when riding in a group, but on my own, I struggle to hold a higher speed. Breaking away is not normally what I do at any point and especially not at the beginning of a ride. When the pace does increase, I never like it to be too early, as I often blow up and get dropped along the way. I was riding well lately, but not well enough to keep working at this rate.

A lot of the riders around me were quite surprised that I had instigated the sudden speed increase. I'm not really known for doing that sort of thing. When I pulled off the front to recover, several comments were made along the lines of 'What's got into you?', 'You're on a mission today' etc. With nearly all of the riders in this group stronger than me, the speed was now never under 35 kmph and often over 42 kmph. With the wind behind us, it was not uncommon to be close to, or over 50 kmph.

While the rest of the group turned off to head for the coffee shop, Max, Steve and Michael had carried on to make up our training time. We had dropped Alex earlier and he had busted his gut to close the gap on us. I had missed the turn off when the group split and found myself suddenly joined by Alex as I turned around to follow the others. Alex and I set out to chase down the boys, but I was simply 'hanging on to his wheel', desperately trying to recover. As those three disappeared from sight, I took a quick sip of fluid, but barely able to breathe, it ended up going down my throat the wrong way. I began choking and spluttering my way to a halt. Exhausted with the work rate we had been doing, I was soon feeding the wildlife as I recovered and waited for the others to come back towards me. I turned around and started accelerating, hooking onto the back as the boys flew past. The five of us headed back to town, the taste of coffee, orange juice or hot chocolate urging us on. With speeds well over 40 kmph we were all only centimetres away from each other's back wheel as we slip streamed our pace line, rotating frequently to keep the speed up and our legs from burning too much.

# The Day It All Went Wrong

Not long after I had commenced my turn on the front, Steve yelled to me that there were riders ahead. Seeing the bikes in front, the speed picked up even more as we set out to chase them down. Checking for traffic, I pulled off the front before I became too exhausted, advising the guys that there was a truck back a bit, but not close enough to worry about. I was soon holding last wheel and made another quick turn to look behind to see how close the truck was from us. I recognised the APH Construction truck in the distance, a vehicle we see nearly every time we ride on the Ironman bike course. Less than 10 km from the end of our two hour ride, we slowed down a little to go through a small roundabout. Splitting the group slightly, I was off the pace a few metres and worked hard to get back into Michael's slip stream. At this same time, Steve had approached the group we had seen earlier, and was moving us right, to overtake them. Approaching Michael, as he was moving right, I overlapped his back wheel slightly and my front wheel connected with it. I tried to ease my bike away as best I could, but being on my aero bars, I didn't have as much control as you normally do when holding onto the main handle bars.

As soon as my wheel touched Michael's wheel, I knew I was in trouble. I had been riding for over 4 years now and experience told me that this was not going to have a happy ending. I screamed to Michael that I was in trouble and gripped the bars as hard as I could, to stay upright. Once Michael's wheel was past mine, my front wheel bounced away instantly, causing me to lose control of the bike and hit the ground as the bike jack knifed. What was worse however was that the truck following us was now even closer! The truck had slowed down to go through the roundabout, but was accelerating again as the driver looked to overtake us.

As I hit the ground, I remember the impact briefly and immediately realised that the truck was not far away and I had to move. I have no idea how much time passed. It may have been 1-2 seconds, or it may have been 4-5. I heard the horn and the brakes as the truck skidded towards me, my bike and I directly in its path. The bull bars of the truck gathered up me and my bike and what followed was the sound of brakes, the smell of burning rubber, the scream of pain and the crunching sound of my bicycle sliding across the tar seal with me still on it, sort of.

I don't know how conscious I was, but was very much awake once the truck finally stopped. I lay out to the side, my right foot pinned by the truck's left wheel. The door opened and the driver jumped out, bent down and saw me lying there. Words may have been spoken, but I can't recall them. I probably politely asked him to move his truck off me!

Being conscious for nearly the entire time, I can recall most of the details that took place, from before I crashed, right through to my arrival at Royal Perth Hospital and beyond. Some parts however, are blank. I think this is for the best! As far as I am aware, everything about my story is correct, based on the information I was told as things happened. There may be slight discrepancies from the medical staff, particularly during the emergency procedures and some of the drugs that were administered, but I'm confident that I have the details as accurate as possible.

As soon as Michael heard me scream, he instantly began yelling to the guys to stop. Not knowing what had happened, they stood together for a few moments wondering who was missing and what had gone on. 'Shaggy's been hit by the truck' Michael screamed and they looked back in disbelief towards the accident scene. Michael was convinced I was dead. 'I'm not going back there,' he said, 'No way', but soon all four of them were around me. The site that greeted them however, was horrific. The skin from around my left thigh had split and peeled back like a banana, from my hip to my knee. It is called a 'de-gloving' injury, as the end result is similar to when you take off a glove - it usually ends up inside out! My femoral artery was exposed and in full view. How this remained intact I don't know, but if it had burst, I may have bled to death right then and there. My left knee had dislocated causing my leg to ragdoll around, which is how most of the damage was done. My pelvis and sacrum broke after the impact of this leg driving itself up into my hip socket. I had two broken bones in my right foot, which was wedged under the front left wheel of the truck.

# The Day It All Went Wrong

Alex appeared out of nowhere and was soon crouched in front of me, talking to me and trying to keep me calm. Michael had called an ambulance, while Max had phoned the police. Steve phoned his flat mate Russell and told him to get out here with Steve's ute, now. If Russell had got there first, they probably wouldn't have waited for the ambulance.

The first thing I remember doing was wiggling my toes. I had movement in my legs and feet, so I knew I wasn't paralysed. This didn't matter to Alex, who gave Steve the job of keeping my head still. Normally an easy task for the in shape, muscle bound athlete he is, but even he had a hard time keeping me under control. Despite their best efforts to stop me, I was looking down at my lower body, but couldn't focus on the injuries. There was lots of blood, my shorts were torn to shreds and I was in a world of pain, mainly due to the twisted position my body was in.

Alex had spent about 10 years with the British Army Marines and even though he had no proper medical training, he had plenty of experience with serious situations. If ever I needed someone like him around, today was the day. Years later we would talk about the accident and how calm he was, but he assured me that on the inside he was anything but calm!

Another cyclist and fellow Kiwi, Jason Hapeta arrived on the scene not long after and came to see what had happened. He kindly offered me his arm and told me to squeeze it, whenever I was in pain. I gladly took up the offer straight away. I lay back waiting for the ambulance to arrive, wiggling my toes every few moments, just to make sure. I closed my eyes and tried not to think too much about what had happened, but as you can imagine, I soon had a million thoughts running through my head.

I don't recall having the 'near death' experience of seeing my life flash before my eyes during the accident. The brain blocking the details as they occurred probably explains this. What I do remember though, were the thoughts I had immediately after everything came to a halt. Thoughts of my family, close friends and others I

## A Long Ride Back

care about and of course, wiggling my toes and moving my legs to ensure they still worked and I could still feel them. I must have done this a hundred times while I was lying there.

The time between when an accident happens and help arriving must be the worst part for those at the scene trying to help. The truck driver was in shock and was being comforted, just as I was being reassured and talked to by my friends. Everyone was trying to remain calm, while desperately wishing help would arrive immediately. Yet despite the seriousness of the situation, there were a few times when the friendship and fun times we had shared together, made it seem like it wasn't as bad as it was. Alex and Steve were trying to make the best out of a really bad situation. As Alex knelt in front of me, he proudly informed me and everyone within a 5 km radius that 'your tackle is in one piece, cos I can see it' in his strong Scottish accent. When the police arrived, my mates were quick to point out that they were both female. 'Are they hot?' I asked. 'Yip, not too bad' was Steve's reply. While I lay there waiting for the ambulance to arrive, I asked Steve why he couldn't just lift the truck off me!' He offered of course, in a way that only Steve could.

Once the emergency services were on the scene, there was debate about whether to move me or wait for a jack to lift the truck off my foot. Luckily, I had convinced Alex that my foot was not trapped it was just pinned under the wheel of the truck. With my neck and back moving freely, the decision was made to get me out from under the rig and into the awaiting ambulance as soon as possible. The paramedic grabbed my foot and yanked it free. Painkillers had been administered by this time but I felt every millisecond of the pain. They pulled me free and lifted me onto the stretcher and then into the ambulance. I probably had more painkillers now as well, so I was soon in a state of calm bliss, while everyone around me began to prepare for the transportation process.

I was rushed to Busselton Hospital where I was quickly assessed, then prepared for departure to Perth via The Royal Flying Doctor Service. Word spread through the cycling community very quickly and while I lay receiving first aid, my friends had the terrible job

# The Day It All Went Wrong

of phoning each other and informing them of what had happened. One of the worst parts about this of course, is that no one knows what is really going on and what information is accurate. Friends had arrived at Busselton Hospital before I had even got there and could only stand around and wait until I was in a condition stable enough to be seen. Inside the hospital, I hardly remember anything that occurred there, except being wrapped in silver sheeting to keep me warm and I'm pretty sure that this was when they put the catheter in, because something hurt a whole lot! The staff there took some photos of me which show my injuries in all their fresh, gory detail. Not many people have seen those particular photos and you won't find them printed in this book.

On my way out the door and into the ambulance to take me to the airport, I was conscious, but very blurry. However, I can remember seeing my friends waiting for me and wishing me well, telling me they would see me in Perth soon.

> *To every man there comes that special moment, when he will be figuratively tapped on the shoulder and offered the chance to do a special thing, unique to him…*
> *What a tragedy if that moment finds him unprepared or unqualified for that work, which could have been his finest hour.*
> **Theodore Roosevelt**

# 2

# Because I Can!

*Far better is it to dare mighty things, to win glorious triumphs even though checked by failure...than to rank with those poor spirits who neither enjoy much, nor suffer much, because they live in a grey twilight that knows not victory, nor defeat.*
*Winston Churchill*

I was not very athletic or sporty as a child, growing up in Taupo, New Zealand. Sure, I ran around like all kids do, but never got into anything seriously. I could always imagine the fantasy of being good at particular sports and often daydreamed of being really awesome, but this was only ever in my head. When it came to actually physically taking part, it was never very impressive. I was familiar with triathlon, having taken part in a team event one year at High School. I bolted the aero bars onto my mountain bike and trained for the 20 km course. Job done; race over; thanks for coming! I had no interest in doing the thing myself, as I had come last in every school swimming event that I was forced to enter. I wasn't a fast runner, so that wasn't going to help much either. Plenty of friends were getting into triathlon and were usually quite good, but it wasn't the sport for me. Riding never continued much outside of High School and although I had thoughts about doing the Lake Taupo Cycle Challenge, it was more fantasy than anything else. This is a 160 km ride around New Zealand's largest lake. The event has grown from strength to strength every year with over 10,000 entrants taking on the rolling hills and undulating countryside in 2011. Way too hard really! So the thought passed, but never fully went away.

Years later, a job opportunity took me from Taupo, New Zealand, to Busselton, Western Australia in 2000. Eating, drinking and not doing very much exercise continued. A 2003 / 2004 world trip kept the belly heading outwards and I returned to Busselton at my heaviest weight ever; 81 kg. Not that heavy for a 27 year old male, but if things continued, soon I would be 85 kg, then 90 kg and then who knows what.

So I started running. Sorry, I could hardly run, so I started walking. Over a few weeks, the running increased and the walking decreased. My boss at the time, Aidan Midgley was in a similar situation to myself, as we would both frequent McDonalds anything from 3-10 times per week. Then, he got a bike. I had a bike, but I didn't used it very often. The idea was there to ride into town every day and get fit, but once I had access to a car, the bike just sat there gathering cobwebs and dust. So I got it out and went riding with him a few times. 15 minutes one way, 15 minutes back. Slowly, the time and distance became greater and it was a bit of fun. A few Corporate Team events at the Busselton Festival of Triathlon in May eventuated from that, but my riding was very ordinary, so there were no great results there. Riding and running continued, but it wasn't for any major purpose, except to try and get fit.

Ironman Triathlon came to Busselton, in November 2004. I knew the format but doing distances of all three that add up to a time longer than most people spend at work each day is another thing! I had watched Ironman New Zealand, thought the competitors were a bunch of stupid, crazy idiots and that was that! Then an old friend from High School, Fiona Docherty told me she was coming to town to race in her first Ironman. So Fiona and her Mum, Irene came to stay and we cheered her on all day as she chased down most of the girls to finish on the podium in second place.

Fiona and her family had always been running and had done many triathlons back in Taupo and around New Zealand. Her younger brother Bevan had just turned professional as well, competing on the ITU World Circuit and had claimed Silver at the 2004 Athens Olympics. He would go on to win bronze in Beijing in 2008 and has his sights set on Gold in London in 2012. Fiona has since turned her focus to marathon running and is also looking to qualify for the London Olympics.

Fiona's day was over after only 9 hours, but most of the other athletes still had anything from 3-8 hours to go. The Ironman cut off time is 17 hours, which is a really long time to be doing exercise for. I watched most of the athletes throughout the day, but eventually got tired, bored and went home. The next night was the after party, which we attended and it was amazing to see how much energy these people had after doing what they had done the day before.

The seed was planted and soon I had thoughts about doing an Ironman myself, one day. Knowing I was a very poor swimmer and hadn't swum since school, I knew I had to get lessons. Aidan had similar thoughts, so off to Busselton's Geographe Leisure Centre we would go each Wednesday night to learn how to swim. After a year of lessons with a number of different teachers we had enough to continue on with. Later that year, we organised another Kiwi friend of ours, Rick Keehan to come across for a working holiday and swim the 3.8 km for us in the 2005 Ironman, John Maclean Teams event. I trained for the 180 km bike ride. Aidan trained for the 42.2 km run and Rick turned up, swam in the pool twice and he was ready to swim. Bastard! Race day came and Rick had us in 3rd position after the swim, which I then dropped to 6th on the ride, while Aidan held on to complete the marathon with a very fractured ankle and we finished 7th. Luckily the 8th team pulled out at the start of the race!

So that was my introduction to Ironman Triathlon. The team's event was only held in Busselton and was a great way to get involved with the Ironman, if you weren't sure about doing the whole thing yourself.

During 2005, I had begun to get involved with The Busselton Triathlon Club and helped form the official status of The Busselton Cycle Club. Through these organisations, I met people who would become very important figures in my life, over the next few years.

## A Long Ride Back

Max and Jenny Higgins, Connie Watson, Michael and Julie Bray, Roger and Wendy Paine, Andy Milne, Louise Leyden, John and Cathy Murrell, Brad and Rosemary 'Purds' Goldsmith, Gary and Wendy Tapper, Peta McAuliffe, Kym and Sharon Nisbet, Jeff and Katie Greenfield, and Steve Anstee to name just a few.

2006 began with my first attempt at the Busselton Jetty Swim in February. This is a non-wetsuit swim and the winner finished in a time of **0:45:22 minutes**. I made it around in **01:36:04 hours**. Then came the Busselton Half Ironman (HIM) in May. I followed a 12 week program from a book called 'Triathlon – An Expert Training Companion', by Mike Finch, which was given to me by Aidan with the words on the inside cover that read:

'Steve, Are you up for the big one! Aidan, Jan 05'.

Apparently I was! I began training, even though I didn't have much of an idea about what I was doing. Despite the distances being half of an Ironman, you only get 7 ½ hours to complete it in and the goal was to be done well before this. A very pleasing swim time deteriorated into two flat tyres on the ride and killing shin splints on the run. Scraping home barely before the cut-off time, I was not happy and would definitely be doing it again next year to get a far more respectable time. The end result looked like this:

**HIM 2006**     – Total - 07:15:20
00:43:01 Swim / 03:55:24 Bike / 02:23:53 Run

After a taste of the long distance triathlons, I decided to take the plunge and compete in my first Ironman event - Ironman Western Australia (IMWA). I followed another program from the same book in preparation for this mental and physical challenge. My race day was a very happy 3.8 km swim, a long, slow 180 km ride and a gruelling 42.2 km run / walk to finish.

**IMWA 2006**     – Total - 13:53:25
01:20:14 Swim / 06:25:32 Bike / 06:07:38 Run

I was only meant to do one Ironman event. I was hoping to be quicker, home in under 12 hours would have been sweet, but was aiming for around 14 hours, so was not too disappointed. For my first event, not knowing what I was doing, how to train, anything about nutrition and other helpful information, I am happy with that result. However, knowing what I know now, I try to make sure first timers find out all they can about what an Ironman entails to ensure they do not finish and think 'I could have done better if....'.

After another short break, it was back into training for the 2007 season. The Busselton Jetty Swim saw me arrive on the sand 45 seconds slower than 2006, in **01:36:49**. All that work and I hadn't improved at all! On to the Busselton Half Ironman after a similar program as the previous year, but more group training and an incident free day saw a remarkable improvement to finish nearly 1 ¼ hours faster than 2006.

**HIM 2007** – Total - 05:58:08
00:39:04 Swim / 02:42:47 Bike / 02:27:09 Run

I was very happy and excited for the next IMWA in December. Yes, crazy me had entered once again, but was smart enough to realise that I needed a lot of help. The dramatic decrease in time between HIM's 2006 and 2007 was really only due to not having two flat tyres. My swim and run times were not far off being the same, two years in a row. This was something I hadn't really realised until gathering the facts and figures for this book. Still, I feel that I would not have ridden anywhere close to the 2007 bike time, based on my fitness in 2006.

My second season of soccer for Busselton's third division continued over the winter of 2007 and I even made it onto the bench for a couple of the reserves team games. Quite a good year for me as I found the back of the net 5, (count them) 5 times, with a double in one game! This is probably the only bit of bragging you will hear from me, as these goals came when most of the results were heavy losses against more fitter and skilful opposition.

Not long after the HIM in May 2007, a training and infor-

## A Long Ride Back

mation night was organised by the Busselton Triathlon Club, and hosted by Ross Pedlow of Exceed Triathlon Coaching, in Perth. Ross gave us a training program and detailed what Ironman was all about. I phoned Ross a few days later and asked him to be my Coach. It was an emphatic 'No' as he was too busy already, was based in Perth and I was 3 hours away in Busselton and he didn't want to, basically. By the end of the conversation, his final words were 'I'll think about it, you think about it and get back to me'. We talked again a few days later and he agreed to coach me, as long as I did everything he asked of me. If not, I was on my own. Fair deal, I thought, so that was that! Training continued and I slowly began to improve in all three disciplines. Race day for IMWA 2007 arrived and it was a new personal best swim time, by 8 minutes. I still couldn't crack a sub six hour ride time, but the run was a personal best (PB) by an hour. All up, it was a big improvement from **13:53:25** in 2006.

**IMWA 2007** – Total - **12:10:10**
**01:12:19 Swim / 06:06:54 Bike / 04:50:56 Run**

We were aiming for less than 12 hours, so despite the 1¾ hour improvement, I thought I had failed. On the phone to Ross, I found myself in tears, apologising to him, because I hadn't gone under 12 hours, like we had planned. His response was exactly what a great Coach should say – 'Don't worry about it. That's Ironman! So what if you didn't finish under 12 hours. You finished! Who cares? I don't and neither should you!'

Now it was time to relax and enjoy a break from training and make the most of the festive season approaching and most importantly, give my body a rest before my next goal. On 01 January 2008, I began training for Ironman New Zealand (IMNZ) and returned home in March to see my friends and family and compete in Taupo. A new swim PB was ruined by a very slow transition, followed by an again average time on the bike. A niggling Illiotibial Band (ITB) injury kicked in straight after the ride and the 42.2 km marathon run was another long afternoon / evening. Ross had taught me to be mentally tougher during IMWA, so the legs kept moving though my knee ached the entire time, even with painkillers. I had run the whole way except for the aid stations and earned another PB. I still couldn't crack the sub 12 hour mark, but the end result was this:

**IMNZ 2008**     – Total – 12:17:07
01:09:34 Swim / 06:10:38 Bike / 04:41:19 Run

After the race was over, the focus then turned to relaxing and enjoying spending time with my family before returning to Busselton in preparation for 2008's HIM. The swimming and cycling continued, but I was very hesitant to run too far as I didn't want to do serious damage before May, as the ITB injury was still hanging around. I spoke to Ross a few days before the event and told him of my plan. 'I haven't run since the first week in April. My swimming and cycling are still going well, so I'm just going to pull something out of my arse on the day!' The race day swim was not as fast as I wanted, but the ride was the easiest I had ever done and seeing all of my friends out competing as well, made it a lot of fun. My plan was simple - swim fast, ride strong and if I blew up on the run and had to pull out, so be it. Pulling out would have really tested how tough I had become, so I'm glad I didn't have to find out. IMNZ was what I had been concentrating on, so this was just icing on the cake, hopefully! The final time:

**HIM 2008**     – Total – 05:27:11
00:39:44 Swim / 02:36:33 Bike / 02:05:56 Run

Where I managed to find a run time like that from I don't know, but I was very happy with my new HIM personal best time. I should point out that this time was still around 1 ½ hours behind the winner. It was pleasing to know that what Ross was teaching me was working. 'Bring on the Ironman,' I thought. 'Sub 12 hour, here we come'.

Another post-race break gave me time to relax and as training resumed later on in the year, I slowly got back into things. IMWA 2008 would be here soon and I would be out to destroy my 2007 time. Nothing was going to stop me from going under 12 hours. Nothing! Little did I know how wrong I was!

*It doesn't take talent, it just takes a decision.*
*Peter Grace*

# 3

# Mind Games

*Nurture your mind with great thoughts, for you will never go any higher than you think.*
*Benjamin Disrael*

My training program began about 16 weeks prior to Ironman Western Australia. Although I didn't foresee it at the start, 2008 was to become my busiest year in recent times. Working full time at Kym Nisbet's Carpet Choice in Busselton, I also began doing freelance sports journalism for The Busselton-Dunsborough Mail, a local newspaper, covering football and soccer reviews. This occupied most of my weekends, particularly Sundays and while it was fine at the beginning of the year, it soon began to take its toll midseason.

As training began, I felt something was missing. I couldn't work out what it was or what was wrong. I was tired sure, but that wasn't really it. Then one day I accepted the reality that I didn't want to do the Ironman. Part of me did. The part that saw the new PB, the finishing chute, the party, but the bit that involved the training and the discipline to stretch and rest regularly didn't. Not long into training, the niggling ITB pain in my right leg came back, which we thought would not occur until further down the track. In my preparation for the HIM in 2008, I had Cortisone injections and an MRI scan in April to see if there was anything serious, as we tried to identify what was causing the knee pain I was getting. I swam, rode, ran and hit the gym occasionally as I got into the program and began to get fitter, but the pain in my knee began messing with my head and soon I doubted everything, including my Coach.

Ross rang me on Friday 26 September 2008, just before the

# A Long Ride Back

Queen's Birthday long weekend. Asking how things were going and we discussed pulling out. If the ITB prevented me from competing, then hard luck. There is always next year! My weekend project was to write down the pros and cons for competing and also for pulling out. Talking to my Physiotherapist, Jeff Greenfield, to get his expert advice and valued opinion, I also had to do the most important thing - sort my head out about what I wanted. The decision was made and once it was, a ton of stress fell off me instantly. I was in! We revised the program so I ran less and increased the bike to compensate. Training continued and was going well. On Monday 13 October 2008, I phoned Ross to tell him how great things were going and how happy I was with the decision I had made. I had a confident feeling that a new, improved time would be achieved on Sunday 07 December 2008. Less than 24 hours after this conversation my training came to an abrupt halt.

*All success begins in the mind.*
*You cannot have victory in reality, until you have victory in the mind.*
***John Fuhrman***

*IMWA 2004 with Fiona Docherty. The seed was planted and I didn't even know it!*

*Photo Credit - Irene Docherty*

*My first proper racing bike which I started riding on both before and after the accident. 20,000 km and still going strong!*

*Photo Credit – Steve Crenfeldt*

*Busselton Jetty Swim 2006. I never had the physique for swimming… or riding… or running!*

*Photo Credit – Jo Wilson*

*Max Higgins & Mick Bray after HIM 2007. Mr Busselton & Mr Invincible both look like they have hardly raised a sweat!*

*Photo Credit – Belinda Higgins*

*Some of the Busselton triathletes posing for a local newspaper shot, while preparing for IMWA 2007 either individually or in teams.*
*Photo Credit – Leonie Paine*

*A local group of cyclists heading out on a Saturday morning training ride.*
*Photo Credit – Leonie Paine*

The morning of IMWA 2007. The classic "deer in headlights" look. Not nervous at all!

*Photo Credit – Belinda Higgins*

Three-quarters of the IMWA 2007 Dirty Dozen – Louise Leyden; Mal Hopkins; Max Higgins; Jeff Evans; Jenny Higgins; myself; Connie Watson and Tineke Hancey.

*Photo Credit – Belinda Higgins*

*IMWA 2007 and one of my favourite sporting photos. As Andy Milne told me "I almost look like I know what I'm doing!"*

*Photo Credit – Leonie Paine*

*IMWA 2007. The armband signifies it's only my first lap…I'm not smiling much after this!*

*Photo Credit – Belinda Higgins*

*Hello ladies! Another one of my favourite photos - Jenny Higgins; Wendy Tapper; Tineke Hancey; Louise Leyden and Connie Watson showing off their IMWA 2007 finisher shirts and medals!*

*Photo Credit - Belinda Higgins*

*IMNZ 2008 with my nephew, Jackson Fletcher joining me for a quick 42 km run.*

*Photo Credit – Steve Crenfeldt*

*After IMNZ 2008, with a photo of the entire family! The first time we had everyone together in a long while.*

*Photo Credit – Steve Crenfeldt*

*Some great friends getting together for dinner in the lead up to IMWA 2008. I was meant to be there, but couldn't make it for some reason... Left to right are Max & Jenny Higgins; Marie & Alex Douglas; Julie and Michael Bray; Kym & Sharon Nisbet; Louis Bray; Andy Milne; Belinda Higgins and Allison Slack.*

*Photo Credit – Alex Douglas*

# 4

# Royal Perth Hospital – Intensive Care Unit

*The most important time for you to believe
is when you have no reason to.*

**Natalie Cook**

One of the last things I remember when leaving Busselton Hospital and being loaded into the ambulance to take me to the airport was my friends who were standing around watching and wishing me well, telling me they would see me soon. Then I found myself on a Royal Flying Doctor flight to Perth. Most of this was a blur, but I do remember being awake for parts of it and talking to the paramedic in the plane a few times, during the trip. I hardly think it was stimulating conversation though and I think it was a plane. It could have been a helicopter or a hot air balloon for all I knew!

When I arrived at Royal Perth Hospital, the condition of my leg was not one that is often seen by most staff. So apparently, I was the talk of the emergency department as they tried to get as many medical personnel to see my injuries as they could, as well as keep me alive of course.

I spent the first few days in the Intensive Care Unit at RPH, while the surgeons attended to me as best they could. When I arrived, my condition was serious, but stable, with injuries as follows:

3$^{rd}$ and 4$^{th}$ metatarsals broken in my right foot, but my toes were fine.

Loss of skin on right side of right foot from the little toe through to the heel.

Major bruising on the sole of my right foot, turning it almost completely black.

My left knee was dislocated, damaging my Anterior Cruciate Ligament.

Nearly complete loss of skin (de-gloving) on my left leg from my hip down to my knee, right around the entire leg. The skin loss includes the inside leg, most of the skin covering the thigh, hamstring, quadricep, right around and under the groin including the join where the leg attaches to the torso.

With the skin, went the flesh and fat underneath it. All hair follicles and most nerve endings were gone too.

My pelvis was broken in two places, one of which was my sacrum.

My sacrum broke when my left leg forced itself about 2½ cm up into the hip socket.

The hip itself did not break, but the force carried through the bones and then onto the pelvis.

There was no damage to my back, neck or spinal cord. There was conflicting information early on about whether my hip was broken, but it was eventually confirmed that it wasn't.

Shortly after being admitted, I had a red band strapped to my ankle and wrist which had my name and patient ID # H8253626. This was a number I would be repeating off hand very frequently. The colour of the band told the staff that I had an allergic reaction to something, in my case Penicillin.

Friends from Busselton, including my girlfriend at the time, Peta McAuliffe; my flat mate, Allison Slack and very good friend, Rosemary "Purds" Goldsmith arrived not long after I did and the visiting procession began. However, because I had no family in Australia, no one was able to see me initially, as visits were restricted to 'family only'. Quick thinking from these three introduced themselves as my wife and two sisters, so they were able to find out what

## Royal Perth Hospital – Intensive Care Unit

was happening, then and through regular updates later on. I don't think the staff at RPH realised what they were in for, as my tally of visitors began to grow from day 1.

When I arrived at RPH, a decision that the medical staff had to make, was whether or not they could save my leg, based on how bad the dislocation was; the damage it had done to my pelvis; the risk of infection associated with the de-gloving of my thigh and the general condition it was left in, with my femoral artery exposed and a lot of the leg tissue gone. I did not know that these discussions were even taking place at the time and was not made aware of this situation until several months later, when attending a post-care review.

Fortunately, the doctors and surgeons felt that my leg was saveable and the priority became replacing the skin around my thigh. Because the skin had de-gloved, a good proportion of it was still attached. It was just hanging off like a banana peel. The doctors were able to cut this off, clean it up, save what they could reuse and freeze it for later on. They managed to save and replace about 70% of this skin. The remainder of skin required, would then come from my right leg, through surgery several days later.

Initial operations on my leg, were to clean the area and ensure no infection got in, while preparing for the skin graft procedures that would follow. As the skin grafts were the most important and delicate operations, nothing much could be done to help fix the broken bones. No metal plates, screws or bolts could be inserted, as this would dramatically increase the chance of an infection and undo any of the work that the plastic surgeons would do. My whole upper left leg was wrapped in a black vacuum dressing from my waist down to my knee, which was connected to a machine which had tubes running from it, into the dressing. These would constantly suck up any unwanted fluid from the wound, as well as keeping a vacuum seal around it so that no infection could get in. With this on, the only option that the Orthopaedic doctors had was to keep me still and put my leg in traction. The first day that I was aware of an operation, was on Friday 17 October 2008. Any surgery before this date occurred when I was in a very happy place, far, far away!

The vacuum dressing on my leg was without doubt the worst part of the whole ordeal. The motor of the vacuum droned loudly all the time, every minute of the day. It felt like the dressing would compress itself onto my leg and then release, for the tubes to vacuum all the unhealthy fluid out of the wound. When it was compressing itself tighter and tighter around my leg, the pain was almost unbearable. It would go in short bursts, so I could tell when the most intense pain was due to arrive, but preparing for this never made it any better. This was the situation I was in and there wasn't much that I could do about it.

Very early on, once I was in a stable condition, I was hooked up to a PCA – Patient Controlled Analgesia, which is where the patients can administer their own pain relief. One push of the button would release a small amount of Morphine into the body. Once pressed, no more medication would be released for 5 minutes; no matter how many times the button was pushed. The details of this were lost on me and I would often be pushing the control much more frequently and would even think I had received more pain relief, when in fact I hadn't. It is strange how sometimes the body thinks you have gotten medication, when it hasn't, only based on what you believe is happening.

A lot of the times, the nurses would get me to push the PCA button and get a hit of pain relief just before they had to move me when changing linen or washing me. This made the moving around much more bearable and I was very grateful for their caring advice with this suggestion.

Information to the outside world became worse, as no details of my condition would be given out to non-family members. I had my 'Sisters and Wife' acting on my behalf, so they were able to find out was going on. Once my real family back in New Zealand found out however, proving that they were still family and finding out what was happening proved to be a nightmare for them over the next few weeks. My flatmate Allison had phoned Rick, back in Taupo and

## Royal Perth Hospital – Intensive Care Unit

asked him to contact Mum and Dad and tell them what had happened. Not easy phone calls for anyone of them to have to make.

I hadn't told my family that I was going out with Peta yet, so the first they ever knew she existed was during this time. The girls were being given regular updates by the doctors and nurses and had to relay this information to my family back home. Luckily this didn't last too long and they were soon able to ring and find things out themselves. As if having a family member involved in a serious accident wasn't bad enough, finding out what was going on through complete strangers was even worse and there were many tears of frustration flowing on both sides of the Tasman.

My memory of the layout of the Intensive Care Unit is very vague, but there are some occasions, where things are very intense and clear, but only for very short amounts of time. I recall a large room, with about 6–8 beds in. With all the patients being critical, it was always a hive of activity and had machines constantly buzzing and beeping with nursing staff trying to take care of a number of patients, all in the same area, with a variety of different problems. Patients were being moved in and out and the doctors and nurses were checking on the patients fairly frequently. There seemed very little space around my bed and the few memories I have of visitors with me, were standing room only and nobody could stay for long.

One of the first memories of being in hospital, included the self-inspection of my body (as much as I could) to find out for myself what state I was in and what damage had been done. I was very confused to discover I had one very smooth, clean shaven left testicle and one untouched and very hairy, right testicle. Obviously the right one wasn't getting in the surgeon's way as much! This had to be seen of course, and lifting up the sheets to see what had happened down below was not a pretty sight, with the bruising and dressings that covered my entire left leg, not to mention the wound on my penis, which made me realise that my injuries were very serious and could have been much worse.

In the first few days after the accident, I didn't really grasp the seriousness of my overall condition and told my visitors that I would be out of hospital in a few days. Luckily, they knew better and just agreed with me, to keep me happy. Crashing on the Tuesday, apparently I was convinced that it wasn't too bad and I would be home by the weekend. I even thought I'd be out in time to still do the Ironman in December. None of the girls wanted to tell me that this would not be possible, so Ross was given the job of informing me that I was not going to be doing the Ironman in Busselton in 2008, or the HIM in May 2009, or the Ironman again in December 2009 either. I did not grasp the seriousness of what he was saying at the time, but I didn't argue, even though I didn't believe him completely.

Ross had drawn a picture on a big piece of paper and brought it in to me in ICU. It was a coloured drawing of a glass, with the water line at halfway. On it, said the following words:

Steve, the glass is half full…and what a great half it is.

Signed Ross – Your Coach

With colouring done by Joshua Finn Pedlow (his son)

This poster was promptly stuck on the wall where I could see it and was moved to a similar location, each time I was moved to another room. This picture still remains on my bedroom door as a constant reminder to stay positive. This is something that is not always easy to do and definitely doesn't always happen. A few months later, Ross would play a major part in a mission that would become the highlight of my hospital stay.

Two days after my first operation, I was back in theatre as the surgeons continued cleaning the wound and tried to reattach portions of skin that they had managed to save when I arrived. Because my leg was in such terrible condition, a lot of work was done just to clean and prepare it for future operations. I don't know the exact date, but on Saturday 18 October 2008, I was in the Major Trauma Ward, so I suspect that I left ICU, the day before.

Royal Perth Hospital – Intensive Care Unit

*A pessimist sees the difficulty in every opportunity;
the optimist sees the opportunity in every difficulty.*
**L. P. Jacks**

# 5

# Royal Perth Hospital – Major Trauma Ward

*The greater the obstacle, the more glory in overcoming it.*
***Moliere***

The Major Trauma Ward (MTW) at Royal Perth Hospital is one of the best in the country apparently, not just for its awesome staff, but for the way it was designed. When the planning began, a lot of staff, including the doctors, nurses, and orderlies were able to give their input as to what they wanted, with suggestions and ideas of what would work. The end result was a Ward that was set up to cater for the staff who actually worked in it. This benefits the patients greatly as the staff are working in an environment that they have helped create and have everything they need at their fingertips, most of the time.

The cycle of visitors began almost immediately after I arrived at RPH's Intensive Care Unit and continued into the MTW. Sometimes it would be one or two visitors and other times we would have ten or more people crowded into the room, much to the nurses frustration. Some of my co-workers from Carpet Choice in Busselton, including Marc Ford, Joel Nisbet and Jeff Coventry were often working in Perth on flooring jobs and would drop in to see me as often as they could as well. Other friends who lived in Perth began arriving to visit, once they were informed of my accident. These included Ross, Tineke Hancey, Lajos Varga, Simon Green, Rob and Glenis Slack, and Darryl McGrath, but I'm sure there were others as well.

The first room I remember, in the MTW was Room I. I think

this was just next to the entrance and the nurses station, which was very handy for everyone. On several occasions, I could hear visitors enquiring about me, so I would just yell out to them until they found me. I'm sure this annoyed the nurses considerably, but that didn't bother me!

Throughout my recovery, we began taking photos of my wounds, in case I wanted them further down the track. Most of these are very gory and very detailed and I look terrible in them. This was a great idea though, as it was useful to see the healing process over the months and is good to look back on, years later.

I have photos with my leg in traction on Monday 20 October 2008, so I assume that this occurred either that day or a few days before hand. A 3 kg bag of water was attached to my leg to slowly pull it back down from the hip socket and relieve the pressure on the sacrum and pelvis. Under my doctor's orders, I was not allowed to lift my upper body more than 30 degrees off the bed and wasn't able to roll over onto my stomach at all. I was only allowed onto my side with assistance, when the staff were either washing me, or changing my bed linen. My leg was positioned between two stiff brace blocks, to stop me from moving my leg left or right. It had to remain as still as possible and I required extra assistance whenever the nurses had to move me.

Lying at 30 degrees, I could hardly even eat properly by myself. I had to have someone cut up my meals for me and even feed me soup on some occasions as I would end up wearing it otherwise. Sharon Nisbet seemed to get the job of cutting up my dinner whenever she visited me in RPH and when she wasn't doing that, she was rubbing moisturising lotion into my feet and massaging them. This is a great feeling at the best of times, but when you can't even reach your toes yourself, having someone do this for you was heaven! My diary tells me that Pat Bromell also assisted me with my meal dissection during their visit in early November. I'm sure that others were involved in this duty as well!

The funniest part about being in traction was the blue tags I had on my wrist and ankle, similar to the red one for my allergy to Penicillin. The blue colour of the tag warned all staff that I was at risk of falling, which made me laugh throughout my time in hospital, as I don't know how I could possibly fall, when I could hardly even move and couldn't get out of bed, even if I tried, especially when they attached the 3 kg water bag to my leg.

Each day seemed to revolve around medication and drugs. I was having 2 Panadol every 4 hours as well as a Tramadol when required. Tramadol is very strong and is used for treating severe pain, so it does the job very quickly. Another painkiller I had was Oxynorm, which contains Oxycodone and is related to Morphine. This was taken on request usually at night when I wanted to sleep, but couldn't because the pain was so bad. When the skin graft operations were all finished, I was given 1 Aspirin twice a day, as this helps the body's healing process, prevents blood clotting and a variety of other functions.

At the accident scene, Morphine was the first drug given to me. This was changed to Pethidine in ICU and the MTW. The first week or so in RPH, I was on a Heparin Drip, also used to prevent blood clots. I had to have a Clexane injection each evening, which is designed to thin the blood and prevent clotting, due to my being bed bound. This was done by injection into my stomach, resulting in more holes and bruises on my upper body, which had otherwise escaped unscathed during the accident.

Having to remain lying down meant that I was in constant risk of my bowel shutting down. Movicol was taken twice a day to help prevent this and keep me 'regular' (or as much as possible). This was a salty, sachet powder, mixed with water, which not surprisingly tasted like seawater. I tried various options to make it better, by mixing it with lemonade, or even milk, but these options were still pretty bad.

Also assisting the bowel was Sorbitol, a clear sugary laxative, given in a small plastic cup, which was kind of like taking a shot of alcohol, but without the headache and hangover the next morning.

Sorbitol is used to relieve any constipation which occurs, mainly from all the painkillers that I was being given.

Another drug I had noted as taking was Memprosal, which apparently doesn't even exist! Tony Best, my GP thinks it may have been Omeprazole which is an antacid medication used for preventing stomach ulcers which sometimes occur when the body is stressed. Being on so much medication and drugs, it's no wonder I was getting some of them wrong, when trying to keep track of what I was taking! I'm sure that the medication I have listed throughout this book is only a handful of what I was administered. It would be impossible to list everything, but the ones I have mentioned are the ones I remember.

One of the questions I was always asked, particularly before surgery, or when identifying me properly for issuing medication, (along with my name, age, today's date, Patient ID #), was if I had any allergies. Informing the staff that I was allergic to Penicillin became quite boring, so I soon changed my answer to Penicillin and trucks. This would always get a laugh from whoever was interrogating me.

For all the drugs I was on and the condition I was in, it amazes me how much I can remember and also, for the people visiting me, how lucid and coherent I was most of the time, particularly at the early stages, in the first few days after the accident. Some things are as clear as anything, but others are just a blur, which makes me wonder if I remember them or dreamt them. One of these memories, which are quite clear, except for the exact room number I was in, occurred in Room I (I think). I was at the back end of the room, with the curtain separating the two beds. In the front half was a guy who had a motorbike accident. He was drunk, speeding and wasn't wearing a helmet. Three out of three for this idiot! How he survived was a miracle in itself, but the abuse he dished out to the nurses and medical staff who were trying to help him was unbelievable. I would lie there unable to believe what I was hearing as this guy was carrying on like a complete loser. I remember acting all tough and wanting to go over and tell him what I really thought of him, but unfortunately I couldn't get out of bed! Boy, he was lucky! I think I used other words at the time to describe him, but I'm sure you all get the gist of what I thought!

There was another couple who had had a car accident out in the desert and had been brought to RPH, but were in separate rooms because of their injuries and hospital policy, I guess. The demands that this guy made to the people who were looking after them were ridiculous. I'm sure it must have been a difficult time for them, probably because they didn't have a tremendous support team around them like I did, but his behaviour was disgusting. It must have been a welcoming change for the nursing staff to get my room, because they had heard how polite and well-mannered I was. Mum would have reached over from New Zealand and slapped me across the back of the head, if she ever heard me carry on like some of those people. Other times were memories of drugged up patients yelling at the staff and Security or the Police having to come and sort them out.

What amazed me with situations like this, and I saw a wide variety of them throughout all of my hospital visits, was how poorly the staff are often treated by patients who they are trying to help. Most of them seemed to be drug or alcohol fuelled, but the way these 'sick or injured' people behaved was often horrible and a poor reflection on society. I always tried to make a conscious effort, when the drugs allowed, by thanking the staff for all they were doing for me. It takes such little effort to show your appreciation for these wonderful people who I strongly feel, do not get paid enough money.

I was often given medical updates and progress reports by the doctors when they did their rounds each morning. Here, I was told information about my condition, but because of the state I was in, it just went right over my head. My phlegmatic nature means I am not a big fan of details at the best of times, but without someone else in the room to take in what was being said, it really was a waste of time telling me anything of importance.

# A Long Ride Back

Being in a hospital like RPH, changes to planned events were always inevitable. One such time was on Thursday 23 October 2008. On this day, my operation was scheduled for mid-morning. However, delays and other emergencies postponed this and I didn't get in until after 2:00 p.m. This meant that I wasn't allowed to eat anything all day as I could have gone for surgery at any moment and you can't eat before an operation – just like going for a swim too, apparently. More visits to theatre occurred on the following Sunday and Friday, to clean the area, ready for the skin grafts to be done.

There was a bit of excitement on the evening of Monday 03 November, when the nurses told me they were moving me into a bigger room. Purds was staying up in Perth for the night and was doing her usual fantastic job of keeping me company. The excitement of a move gave her an opportunity to 'sort out and tidy' my room. Everything had a place as far as Purds was concerned and she would often come in to visit and complain about how messy things were when she had only left the night before! At some other point over the past few weeks, I had been moved to Room H, for whatever reason, but with this second move, I was now in Room F, where I would stay for the rest of my time in RPH. These room changes would surprise a few of my friends who were expecting me to be in one room, but were then told I wasn't there. Even the doctors and medical staff got caught out by this a couple of times. Room F was much larger and had a massive window, with a really wide windowsill, perfect for storing my cards, flowers, chocolates and other possessions. I really think that recommendations were made by the staff to move me into this room, as apparently it was one of the biggest and best in the Ward. The reward for being a fabulous patient, obviously!

The next day, I was scheduled for another operation. I was fasting and waiting to be taken through. Around 3:00 p.m. I was informed that there was not enough time to perform the skin graft, so they would cancel me for today and try again tomorrow. This was very frustrating and extremely annoying. The only positive on this day, was when one of the nurses offered to wash my hair for

## Royal Perth Hospital – Major Trauma Ward

me. I was unable to shower or bath since the crash, so having this simple task done for me, was wonderful. Head massages are great at any time and the gentle motion of washing my hair was much better than surgery.

The time between my visitors getting kicked out, often after 9:00 p.m. usually after visiting hours were long closed, through until around 7:00 a.m. when breakfast was normally brought in was the hardest time. In fact, it was the worst time. The vacuum dressing compression bandage that was wrapped around my left leg was noisy and painful and droned constantly. I tried to find things to do to occupy myself on the occasions that I was awake all night. Trying to be productive as the hours crept along was exhausting in itself, but hardly ever enough to wipe me out for the entire night. The hours dragged and sometimes I would wake, thinking I had slept through, only to discover that only an hour or two had passed. Other times I would just get to sleep and would be woken by the night staff who had to turn me, to prevent bedsores. The orderlies would come around to turn the patients who were unable to move themselves. This was a painful process and was also very limited to the traction and the wound on my backside from where the initial skin graft testing site was done. On most occasions I would ask them not too, but only rarely did they miss me. They had their job to do, regardless of the pain it caused unfortunately, and what they did was for the best in the long term, even though the patient never understands that at the time.

Watching television during the midnight hours was one of the main activities I would do. This often resulted in watching the same movies fairly often, but never actually seeing the whole thing entirely from start to finish. Even now, I might be watching a movie and get the feeling I have seen certain scenes, but don't recall ever watching it. It's usually one that I saw in hospital, exhausted from lack of sleep and drugged up to my eyeballs.

On Wednesday 05 November, the operation eventually took place, as the surgeons transferred layers of skin from my right thigh to my left thigh and reattached the rest of the layers that had peeled

## A Long Ride Back

back during the accident. These layers were cut off when I arrived and kept frozen until the doctors were ready to use them. Amazing when you think about it really! After this operation, my legs were wrapped in gauze, with dressings and bandages, resulting in my two thighs looking like a mummy!

I don't recall being nervous or apprehensive about any of the early operations, I guess because I wasn't my normal self. It was very surreal, but even that is not an accurate description really. Unless you have experienced it yourself, you may struggle to understand what I mean. The best part about the earlier operations was that I didn't realise the seriousness of it all. Even though I was told what my injuries were, I didn't really understand exactly what it all meant. Also, being so drugged up on pain relief, it was basically just laying back and getting fixed. I didn't have any say in it and didn't really have too much time to think about things in the first few weeks. I can't even say that I just did what I was told, as I didn't have a choice on anything. It was just lie there and take it!

The next day, I was left with not just one sore leg, but two, very sore legs. The skin grafts were completed and the black vacuum dressing had been removed finally. It was a great relief to have this gone and with it the noisy motor and the painful vacuum of it compressing around my leg. I cannot explain how grateful I was to have this off, and can confirm that it is true what they say, that the donor site hurts more than the actual injury!

On Friday 07 November, the dressings were changed and the doctors saw that **95%** of the grafts had taken. The surgeons were thrilled and everything was going well. There was nothing more the surgeons could do for now, I just had to rest and recover and let the healing process begin.

The dressing change on the Sunday, two days later, was the first time I actually got to see my leg since the accident. When I looked down and saw it, I had a lot of trouble accepting it. It just wasn't my leg. It looked like a massive lump of Scotch Fillet Steak, with a knee, lower leg and foot attached. The Doctors, Nurses and

Surgeons were always pleased with what they saw, but I was not. There was nothing positive that I could see. It looked horrible and I hated it. I also knew that it would look like that for the rest of my life. I desperately wanted it to look like it used to, or even to end up looking like my right leg, the donor site, but that was never going to happen. The anger and frustration I had at this time, cannot truly be described in a way that you would understand. I was more than angry, it was hatred almost. Here, I actually had thoughts about asking to have the leg removed, so then I wouldn't have to see it. I can't even write words to share exactly how I felt – and this is three years later! I would entertain thoughts of having it amputated and then dealing with either nothing at all, or a prosthetic replacement, though this didn't really seem like a great alternative either. The medical staff were reassuring me that it will look better over time and I would get used to it. Eventually, I guess I had to believe them and so began the slow process of acceptance, even though it was reluctant.

I had full function of my right leg, but due to the broken bones in my foot, I couldn't put any pressure on it, and now that my right thigh was the donor site, I had restricted, minimal movement here as well. Both legs were painful and I could really only move my left foot by wiggling my toes or rotating my ankle a little.

On Tuesday 11 November, I was told by the Orthopaedic doctors that I would be in traction for eight weeks. What I didn't clarify, was whether that was eight more weeks or a total of eight weeks, from when it began. This uncertainty would lead to much frustration further down the track.

It was 35 days in hospital, until I was allowed to have a real shower, on Monday 17 November. This however, consisted of a 'shower trolley' which I was moved onto and wheeled into the bathroom. Lying there naked, the water hose was handed to me to go about my business. It was definitely a little weird having a nurse in the bathroom with me, but once she offered to shampoo and condition my hair, I was grateful for her presence. She was cute too, so that was always a bonus! Sponge baths are never as exciting as society often depicts and the sexy, buxom nurse rubbing a soapy sponge over your body is as far from reality as you could possibly get. Still, the same jokes never fail to impress and the same definition is always referred to whenever the subject was mentioned by my visitors. My friends are so mature! That would be the only shower I would have, over the 42 days in RPH. My notes state that from today, I had four weeks to go in traction.

Being on so many drugs meant that I was sleeping most of the day, or being so exhausted that all I wanted to do was sleep, but being in so much pain meant that I often couldn't sleep, regardless of how tired I was. It was another frustrating and annoying situation in which there wasn't much I could do. During these times, when I couldn't sleep through the pain, I would plan things to do whenever the PCA was pushed to relieve the pain. These were things such as move around in bed to get comfortable again (as much as I could with a 3 kg bag of water tied to my leg and not allowed to raise my body more than 30 degrees); or reach to pick up things I wanted or needed, again, as best I could.

The drugs I was on caused some very strange and weird dreams while in hospital, but nothing that was too scary or frightening. I recall waking up after many nights like these, but there was never anything too vivid to recall the exact details of. A lot of the times there were dreams which occurred during the day sleeps. Often I would still be so groggy when waking up, that trying to think about what I had been dreaming of was too exhausting in itself and would inevitably send me back to sleep. It was a no win situation.

There was always uncertainty of when the traction would end and the bag of water would be removed from my foot. It seemed that each of the medical staff had their own version of when this would happen, but the decision could only be made by Orthopaedics, and in particular, my Consultant – Gavin Clarke. While I was in traction and the focus was on dealing with the skin grafts of my leg, I felt like I wasn't really much of a priority to the Orthopaedic doctors. I hardly ever saw these guys and was often asking when they would be back to update me. They had no current information to

## Royal Perth Hospital – Major Trauma Ward

share until sufficient time had passed, but I wanted to know what date the traction would be removed. There was confusion over how long this would be. Early reports said 6 weeks, and then it went to 8 weeks, then on to 10 weeks. I wanted a definite date to look forward to and wasn't getting any answers.

There was an occasion after one of my operations, when the needle in my arm was incredibly annoying, so I decided to just rip it out. Not the best idea I have ever had, as the end result was me covered in blood, looking like a victim of a B grade horror movie. I passed out not long afterwards and got a stern telling off by the nurse who had to clean up the mess and try to get the needle back into my arm. We often joked throughout my time in the MTW, that even though I had no injuries above my waist from the accident, the nurses did more damage sticking me with needles every day.

The majority of patients, who have to remain in bed for long periods, are required to wear TED Stockings. These are long white socks which serve a number of purposes including keeping the feet warm and the blood circulation flowing. I found these most uncomfortable as I was very rarely cold and could only have them on one leg anyway. There were a few arguments with the nurses who said I had to wear it, and often I would give in to shut them up and take it off as soon as they left the room.

Sometime near the beginning of the operations, possibly before the skin grafts were started, the surgeons had to choose a donor site to test how durable the skin was to transfer. The location that was selected was my right buttock. I don't know why this area was chosen for a patient who had to spend all of his time lying on his back. Apparently whoever tested this area had the blade on the grafting machine set incorrectly and the layers of skin they removed were much deeper than they should have been. This area didn't have a dressing put on it, a lot of the time, so there was constant pain from laying on yet another wound. For some reason, and again being so drugged up the details are a bit sketchy, but my buttock was an area that was always forgotten about by the nurses. I remember several occasions when there wasn't even a bandage or anything put over it. This meant that whenever I had the bed linen changed, if I wasn't fast enough to lift myself off the sheet gently, it would be ripped off, as it was stuck to my skin, from the blood dripping from the wound and drying. This seemed to be an ongoing problem and anything I tried to say about it, wasn't given the proper consideration. My groggy state didn't help the communication process either! This problem began while I was in ICU and continued on into the MTW. It was only after I managed to convince one of the nurses that something really needed to be done, that she had a look, saw what the problem was, got some advice as to what would be the best option for it and put a dressing on. The wound was one of the slowest to heal and continued to cause problems even after I had left hospital, months later.

Before the crash, I was weighing 73 kg, which I was trying to get up to around 75 – 80 kg. Within the first week in hospital, I lost 14 kg, and was down to 59 kg. I was just about skin and bones as my muscle mass just disappeared and my face looked pale and gaunt. Luckily, whenever my friends would come to visit me, they would all tell me how great I looked or that I was better than last time, so I wasn't too aware of my physical state.

Being bed bound, getting me weighed was quite an experience, as I had to be transferred onto a canvas sling, which was attached to a crane like / Jordan Frame device. I was then lifted up off the bed and weighed. The scales then recorded how heavy I was, less the weight of the apparatus. This only took place on a couple of occasions, but each time, the hospital Nutritionist would arrive the next day and tell me how worried they were about my weight. I was eating as much of the hospital food as I could tolerate and getting plenty of chocolate and other snacks in as well.

I was put on a high protein diet and was eating chicken or turkey for most meals, having milkshakes for lunch and plenty of fruit, but I wasn't building any muscle. I was drinking Sustogen and Arginade to help increase weight, as well as aid the wound healing process. As my condition improved, the weight slowly began to increase, but never to a satisfactory level that pleased the staff. On

Royal Perth Hospital – Major Trauma Ward

Sunday November 16 2008, I weighed 60.8 kg. I was convinced that once I was out of hospital; eating proper, tastier meals and doing physical activity, the weight would be back on quite easily. Trying to get the medical staff to understand this was another story.

*Some of the world's greatest feats were accomplished by people not smart enough to know they were impossible.*
**Doug Larson**

# 6

# Visiting Hours Are Between 8:00 a.m. and 8:00 p.m.

*The things that matter most, should never be at the mercy of the things that matter least.*
**Goethe**

Peta was up to visit me most days and nearly every weekend as well. It was fortunate that she was often able to grab a lift with others who were coming up from Busselton or she would drive to Bunbury and jump on the train. Regardless of how she got there, Peta was in to visit as often as she could and probably used up all of her leave entitlements from work, visiting me. This must have been a frustrating time for her as well, visiting someone who was so drugged up that stimulating conversation just didn't exist, even when I was awake on the rare occasion. Still, Peta did what was needed and not visiting was never an option, as far as she was concerned.

So between Peta, Purds, Allison and Aidan, I had a small army of supporters who were growing every day and would get me just about anything I needed. On Tuesday 21 October, I was complaining because it was too hot and I couldn't sleep. Purds was on the case and brought in a small fan that we attached to my bed frame to keep me cool. Just one example of the lengths my friends went to, to make me as comfortable as possible. Purds' mother Margaret would also visit regularly and kept my supply of Coco Pops cereal stocked up. These were a tasty treat and a delicious change to the porridge, toast or corn flakes that was rotating each morning. Don't judge me - I had to put weight on somehow and they do have 5 Vitamins and Iron, you know!

## A Long Ride Back

One of the earliest visitors within the first few weeks of being in the MTW was a lady called Debbie Burwood, from Busselton. We didn't know each other, but she had worked with Sharon Nisbet. Debbie was currently working at RPH, in another area of the hospital, and called in to see me on several occasions. Unfortunately, each time she came in, I would have no idea who she was or even remember that she worked at RPH, so Debbie would politely reintroduce herself and remind me that she was checking up to report back to Sharon. Even though it was frustrating not knowing this lady and feeling bad that I couldn't remember her at first, it was lovely that she took the time to visit, as she knew how important I was to people in Busselton, particularly Mrs Nisbet.

I never saw Debbie again, once I left RPH, until nearly 3 years later, when I was writing the final few parts of this book. We met up for a chat one afternoon and it was great to finally thank her in person for the visits she made to me while I was in RPH. Whilst I didn't recognise her at first, the more we talked, the more her friendly face and caring smile took me back to the times in hospital. I have no idea what we talked about back then, but it was good to update her on my progress and let her know what I had accomplished since the accident. I just wish I had taken the time to thank her sooner, rather than later, even though she feels she didn't really do anything. Just calling in to visit, was more than enough, thank you Deb!

The gifts and cards soon began to mount up, along with a steady supply of chocolate. I would hate to think how many kilograms of chocolate arrived during my hospital stay, but it was a lot. I ate most of it too! Books, photos, posters, games, flowers, balloons, magazines, fruit, more chocolate and get well cards were all over my hospital room. My boss, Kym loaned me the work laptop and my friends arranged a USB Wireless Internet connection for it. This gave me contact with the outside world and more importantly, I could begin writing email progress updates for those who were unable to visit or lived outside of Australia.

Among the massive array of gifts and other items I received

## Visiting Hours Are Between 8:00 a.m. and 8:00 p.m.

during my time in hospital, were a couple of things that would go on to have significant meaning for me from that point on. First was the drawing from Ross, reminding me that the glass is half full. Second was a massive collage poster, done by Belinda Higgins and Allison, with pictures of myself and my friends, from the past few years.

My bed in Royal Perth Hospital had a frame around it, which could be used for other forms of traction; patients to hoist themselves up with when they were getting out of bed; and also for tying stretchy bands to, for physiotherapy exercises. This framework was useful, as the poster could lie flat on top and I could see it while lying on my back. When Max, Jenny and Belinda came to visit and gave this to me, I was so overcome with the emotion of seeing such an awesome gift, that I was soon bawling my eyes out, with Jenny and Belinda not far behind. Mr Busselton doesn't cry, but I know Max was moved by this situation, nonetheless! This was a very thoughtful idea and the poster is still stuck on my bedroom door and I pause to look at the photos nearly every day.

On another occasion, Debbie Jecks dropped by with her daughter Claire. I had never met Claire before, but she knew all about me, of course. Debbie is another lovely and very creative lady who brought two photo collages in for me. One was a collection of photos of my Ironman and Half Ironman races in previous years, with the words, 'Good Luck Shaggy' written across it. The second poster was photos of nearly everyone in the Busselton Cycle Club and Triathlon Club, either competing or socialising in some form. Again, this was another reminder of how supported I was by all of the friends I had, who cared about me.

I don't know the exact date, and I think it was in the MTW, as opposed to ICU, but a guy came to visit me and introduced himself as Marcel. He explained that he worked at RPH and was the Psychologist assigned to me. He was there for me to talk to and offer counselling if I required it. Professionally, it was to check that I was alright upstairs and that I wasn't becoming overwhelmed and depressed with my situation. Most of these conversations were recorded and I hadn't really thought much about them, until I had nearly finished writing this book. Thinking back now, I can hardly imagine what I would have said to him and I'm sure most of these conversations would have been very strange. They would have been interesting to listen to and no doubt provided additional information for this book.

Unfortunately, the enquiries I made with RPH to get copies of the recordings, led to me finding out that Marcel had since moved on and the recordings had been deleted. Not surprising after 3 years, and something that I should have followed up on long ago. I do remember though, that it was very beneficial to talk to a third party who was not emotionally involved and who I could tell anything to and know that it would not be repeated. Marcel always seemed satisfied that I was not in any real danger of slipping into depression and based on my massive support network I would get through things relatively okay. At a post-care review several months later, with various medical professionals, it was Marcel who informed me of the dilemma the doctors had when deciding whether to amputate my leg or not. This was the first time I had learnt this information and needless to say, it came as a bit of a shock. I am glad that I wasn't aware of this at the time as I doubt that I would have been able to process the information or cope with the potential outcome based on my condition.

During the first week in the MTW, as I became a bit more aware of things, I began asking questions about what had happened on the day of the accident, when I was being taken to Busselton Hospital and eventually on to RPH. Kym had rung a mutual friend of ours, Andy Milne and told him what had happened. They then drove out to the accident scene in Kym's work van and collected my bike, helmet, shoes and what was left of my clothing. A small altercation getting into the closed off accident scene didn't eventuate into much, luckily, as these two were quite fired up about the situation through worrying about my welfare. Kym's wife Sharon washed my cycling gear and managed to remove all of the blood stains so they were looking clean and smelling fresh. She was unable to do anything about the ripped to shreds condition they were in though!

## Visiting Hours Are Between 8:00 a.m. and 8:00 p.m.

At the conclusion of the ride on the Tuesday morning, most people returned to the Samovar Restaurant & Café, where we would regularly meet after this training session. My friends just sat around, not saying too much, as most were in a state of shock and didn't know what else to do. From there, the phone calls began to notify other people of what had happened. Again, not the phone calls that any of them wanted to make, but these helped form the beginning of the support network that I would become so reliant on for many months to come.

Word began spreading through town about what had happened and like the bush telegraph, a variety of versions quickly eventuated. Apparently I was dead already, according to some reports! There was peace of mind for those at the hospital shortly after, as one of the nurses came out to update them on my condition. They were informed that although I was in a serious condition, I was not in danger of dying and I would be alright. Hearing these words had different meanings to everyone, but for Aidan and Purds in particular, they knew that they didn't have to worry unnecessarily and began to set the wheels in motion for what needed to be done on my behalf.

One thing I became obsessed about as I began understanding what took place while I was being attended to, was the orthotics I had in my cycling shoes. These had just cost me $500.00 and I had to ensure they were safe! So here I am, nearly killed in a cycling accident, after wrestling with a truck; having destroyed a bike valued at several thousand dollars and I am worried about a set of orthotics worth a few hundred bucks! Go figure on that! Just one example of the weird way I was thinking on some occasions.

The time difference to the Eastern States and New Zealand was one positive to the frustrating hospital situation I was in, as I could start sending text messages to friends and family, once 3:00 a.m. arrived as it was already 7:00 a.m. in New Zealand and most people were up and starting their day. Writing email updates were also done at night when I couldn't sleep, but I often had to edit them constantly as writing in an exhausted state meant words were spelt wrong or the sentences jumped all over the place like a kid on red cordial. Having always loved writing, sending out updates of my progress was very enjoyable and I tried to ensure they contained plenty of things to keep people laughing, rather than just concentrating on the seriousness of my injuries and condition.

Sometime early on in my hospital stay, the girls discussed getting a book or diary to record who came to visit and other important information. Exactly who turned up with the product itself was a mystery to me, but I think Allison gets the credit for this and I am very grateful that she did. This makeshift diary was started on around Monday 20 October 2008, and was backdated to the day of the accident, as the girls filled in the details, which I was oblivious to. Most of the records were very loosely based on who saw me on what days; visitors; well wishes; phone messages; gifts etc. It was hoped that the medical staff might write down important information that I was too out of it to understand or remember, when no one else was around, but this was in vain.

I had another small notebook given to me early on, probably towards the end of October, which I would use to write down questions for the doctors and also try to keep a list of names of the medical staff I saw and what their role was. Being in the ICU and MTW of Western Australia's busiest hospital, this was easier said than done. Added to each name was a word or brief description to describe each person or their role. It worked for most of them, but in the end, I saw way too many people to count or remember and I was trying to do this while on some serious drugs.

Also in the notebook, were things I would jot down, usually when I couldn't sleep, but often when I was doped up on the good stuff. Not sleeping became very frustrating, as usually it was the vacuum dressing churning away all night, which would keep me awake. With nothing else to do but lay awake and be so aware of it, the hours between 9:00 p.m. and breakfast were very, very hard. The things I would write down were designed to keep me positive, but in reality, I was not interested in doing them. All I wanted was a pain free sleep through until the morning. It didn't happen very

Visiting Hours Are Between 8:00 a.m. and 8:00 p.m.

often! These are the phrases I had written down to 'help' me:

'Every hour awake is an hour closer to removing the pressure bandage'

'Every day that passes will get the skin grafts ready and working'

'Patience! Just lie there and do nothing. Rest.'

If that's not obvious that I was on drugs, I don't know what is! Of course, I was kidding myself with these statements, but everyone kept telling me to stay positive and I would get through it. Being positive is one thing, but lying in a bed with a 3 kg weight tied to your leg, barely able to move without assistance was not even really living. I was simply existing! For me, it wasn't about positivity. It was simply a matter of waiting until I reached a stage where I was allowed to do more. There was no point fighting it, getting annoyed, or even worrying too much about it. That was the situation I was in and for now, there was nothing I could do to change it. Not getting annoyed was very hard, but throwing my toys out of the sandpit would not have helped anyone – especially when I couldn't get out of bed to pick them up!

I don't remember exactly when I did it, but early on in my recovery, I wanted to display the goals I had for everyone to see and give me a constant reminder of what I was aiming for. I took a piece of A4 paper, and wrote the following, in big capital letters:

I AM WALKING OUT OF HERE ON
01 DECEMBER 2008

I WILL BE WATCHING THE IRONMAN ON
07 DECEMBER 2008

THE GLASS IS HALF FULL AND
I AM GETTING BETTER EVERY DAY!

This page was put up on the wall, for me and everyone to see. The walking bit was all just a wish, as I had no idea whether this was even possible or not. The medical staff knew this wasn't going to happen and most of my friends knew that as well, but I think I

## A Long Ride Back

was hoping to be or have some miracle occur that suddenly had me up doing it. Getting out to watch the Ironman on 07 December was also not very likely, but at that time, I still had not grasped the seriousness of my condition. Sometimes though, that can be a good thing. The final statement was an adaptation of the poster that Ross had done for me, which was also on display.

I'm sure my Case Manager, Sheryl Jonescu got sick of me asking whether or not I'd be able to get out in time to watch the Ironman. I don't recall her ever saying no, but she told me that it would depend on my improvement and what the doctors said. I must have bugged her about it a thousand times, but she handled all of my requests in the same professional way, never promising anything and reassuring me that if it was at all possible, she would do everything she could to help.

As November drew to a close and it looked like my goal of walking was not going to happen on 01 December, I changed the date in my head to 06 December, which is my Mother's birthday. That might be a nice present for her I thought, but again, it was just a wish. Getting out in time to watch the Ironman was looking less and less likely as well.

It turned out that I was nowhere near this date when it came to eventually walking, but again, I had no concept of the seriousness of what had happened to me. And some days, even as I began to write notes and ideas for this book, I had to stop and remind myself that it wasn't really that long ago that I was flat on my back in a hospital bed with a 3 kg weight tied to my foot. That is something I think I will be reminding myself of for a while longer.

*It is literally true that you can succeed best and quickest by helping others to succeed.*
**Napoleon Hill**

# 7

# Ironmen Don't Cry – Yeah Right!

*Accept the challenges, so that you may feel the exhilaration of victory.*
**General George S. Patton**

Not long after I moved from ICU to the Major Trauma Ward, I was on the phone to Joel Nisbet, who is Kym and Sharon's son. I mentioned that I had spoken to his mum a few days earlier and he laughed as he said that she would have been crying more than she was talking. She had been crying of course, which meant that I was too. Joel and I had a laugh about this as well and I told him that if anyone gives me shit for crying like a girl, I'd be sending them his way. 'Sweet as' was his reply and I felt a sense of relief that no one was judging me for being an emotional, crying mess, but if they were, he would have a polite word in their ear. It was as though I now had permission to show emotion and I was free to let the tears flow whenever I wanted to.

I hadn't had too many days of feeling down or upset in hospital. For the first month there were only about four times when I got the blues and it all became a bit too much to handle. Not bad for me really. Sunday 09 November 2008, which I named 'Black Sunday' was about the worst, as it was the first day that I had no visitors. I had been bragging about how fortunate I had been with all the friends who had been in to see me lately, so that will teach me! That evening I got a bad dose of cabin fever and the smallest thing that seemed hard set me off with more water works than Niagara Falls in spring. I had seen my wounded leg the day prior, but hadn't paid much attention to it. It looked weird, a bit like steak at the butchers shop and it was hard to believe it was my body in that state, so

## A Long Ride Back

I guess I just figured that that was what it would be like until they fixed it up.

The next morning was the first day that it was redressed and I got to see it clearer and in more detail. This really hit me hard and soon the tears were flowing as I thought about all the negatives associated with it and how I wouldn't be the same again. When one of the Plastic Surgeons came to inspect it, it didn't help when he was telling me how good it looked and began pointing out the areas of new skin and all the positives about how quickly it was healing. Clearly he was wrong and I was right, which got me going yet again!

The best description of my leg at this point is the video clip from Robbie William's 'Rock DJ' song, where he rips his skin off to expose the flesh, before eventually becoming a skeleton. Another is the 'muscle chart' often displayed in gyms, hospitals, and doctor's surgeries, which shows the dark red colour of the muscles on the body. This was very close to what my leg looked like at the time.

As the days in traction continued, I got more and more frustrated. I was still getting great support from my friends, which was vital to keeping me happy and smiling and not dwelling on the condition I was in. Early on in my recovery, I read the biography of Crowded House - Something So Strong. The end of the book describes the breakup of the band and even though I knew the outcome, I found myself crying, at the sadness of my favourite band falling apart, but in a way, it really was quite therapeutic for me to let some feelings out without feeling sorry for myself in the process.

Anyone, who knows me, knows that I am not a tough guy. At 5'10" and around 75 kg, I don't really go around letting my mouth write cheques that my fists can't cash. I'm not sure why I wasn't screaming or even crying more when the accident happened, but I guess shock is a funny thing. I don't consider myself tough to get through any of this ordeal. I was simply doing what needed to be done, every day for as long as it takes. And if that includes crying into a friend's arms, then that was what I did. Many visitors told me

## Ironmen Don't Cry – Yeah Right!

I didn't need to be so strong and not to hold so much in. I never thought that I was until that Sunday with no visitors and only one phone call, when I realised I had been holding too much in right from the beginning. Funnily enough it was an episode on the bedpan later that night that brought me crashing down to reality and everything that was held in emotionally, came flooding out over the fact that I couldn't even do a poo properly.

> *A champion is someone who gets up when they can't.*
> ***Jack Dempsey***

# 8

# Bedpans And Pee Bottles
## Not to be read during meal times!

*Thinking is the hardest work there is. That's why so few people engage in it.*
**Henry Ford**

This occasion on Sunday 09 November, when my body finally released after 4 days of constipation resulted in me sweating, panting and puffing, trying to do 'the job' up until then. All the effort resulted in back spasms ripping through me, a sensation I had never felt before, and one that scared the shit out of me - excuse the pun.

Naturally, being bed bound, if eating and drinking were done in bed, then peeing and pooing were done there too. The pee bottle is obviously easy to manage and rather handy. But lying down for so long means that the bowel doesn't have the usual flow through as you would when walking around. So usually it would fill up until a stomach cramp told you that action needed to be taken. Preparations were made with the required assistance to get me into the appropriate position. This time however, things weren't happening as naturally as they should and so with no action taking place, alternatives were called for.

Unfortunately I was able to experience all types of relief from the classic 'suppositories' to the magical 'Fleet'. Once this thing is up your butt, the evacuation process begins and continues. Just when you think it is all over, suddenly the stomach will groan and then the next wave exits the body. I only had this once luckily and I think that every last ounce of shit was removed from my bowel on this occasion. I didn't think my body could store this much actually, but apparently it could!

It was definitely weird being a 32 year old man and having to have someone wipe your backside. What made it worse was being 'semi-able bodied' with full function from the waist up, but not able to get out of bed. Pooing in a pan is not a nice thing to have to experience, but the key word is 'have'. When you don't have a choice, there is nothing you can do, despite how embarrassed and degraded you feel. Again, the nurses' professionalism makes this experience a little bit easier to deal with, but at no time did it ever become natural or feel any less uncomfortable or less humiliating. It was often made worse at the start, when I needed 2 or 3 other nurses to roll me onto my side and hold me till the job was done. Not much fun for any of the people involved.

So as I lay there crying while a nurse wiped my backside, one of them asked when I had last been outside. As soon as I revealed that I had never left the building since I arrived, he quickly began organising me a roof visit. I could not even contemplate how this was possible, being on traction and unable to move very much. However, I was in for a pleasant surprise. The nurses simply rearranged the tubes coming from my body and unplugged any unessential cables that I didn't need at the moment. Then they pushed my bed out through the door, down the corridor and into the elevator. Up onto Level 6, there is a balcony where all the patients and staff go to have a cigarette. Normally an environment like this is not the ideal place to go to, but the area is big enough to get your own space away from the smoke and enjoy the fresh air and relative freedom, as well as seeing a bit of a skyline view of Perth city.

This was repeated the next day and few times after that, with the visitors I had getting to enjoy the experience as well. The escape from cabin fever and being bed bound came at exactly the right time and got me comfortable enough to survive the rest of my time at RPH indoors. One of the best things with this was that I could be left up there and would just ring the Ward when I wanted to go back and the staff would come and get me. It was a win / win situation, as they didn't have to keep checking on me and I had a very limited feeling of some normality.

Any dignity I thought I had was taken away by the truck, on the day I crashed. As I looked down at my legs, I could see my penis and testicles covered in blood, but still attached, by the look of them. I remember Alex joking as he told me that they were safe, because 'we can all see them!' The old fella didn't escape unscathed however and I now have a decent size scar to remind me how close I came to losing him. No stitches required fortunately, but it was quite a deep gash and a bit too close for comfort really! This of course made for plenty of jokes amongst the guys when visiting me in hospital and also months later.

Being in ICU and as high as a kite for the first few days, I had no idea who had seen me naked, but can guess that a lot more people had than I knew. Being in such a condition with the nurses having to take care of you, nowhere is out of bounds really. Thankfully the majority of them are professional enough to make you feel quite relaxed about things, but when a doctor cruises in with his seven or eight person medical entourage, you generally found yourself reaching for anything to cover up with, as clothes were rarely on me, most of the time.

The humorous side of things eventually came out when the bathroom habits would inevitably have to be shared with any roommates you had. We would often laugh at how the doctors and nurses would pull the curtain closed to discuss things, give injections or deal with the bathroom issues, when the patients would freely discuss these things in open conversation once they were gone. On one occasion at RPH, the guy next to me couldn't piss and I couldn't poo, so we had to laugh at what a useful combination we made.

Fast forward several weeks to Shenton Park and a room of four patients. The one uniting thing with all of us in the room was usually you had all experienced the constipation and knew what it felt like. There were often celebratory yells and cheers when success

## A Long Ride Back

was finally reached and the relief was experienced. Of course all the trying that went on made for some beautiful arse music, which was welcomed and praised by the patients, but shunned and disgusted by the nurses. The more people that come to realise that farts are funny and the louder and longer they are the better, then the world will be a much happier place to live! I even had bragging rights one day at SPRC, when I had to call for another pee bottle, because I had filled the first one up and was still going strong!

Having experienced Fleet back in RPH, when my bowel shut down, I would kindly offer it as a suggestion to other patients in my room at Shenton Park, who were in a similar situation. As this is usually the last option, the nurses knew what I was referring to and it was a bit of fun teasing the other patient's as they had had all sorts of ideas running through their heads as to what I was talking about.

*Genius is one per cent inspiration and ninety-nine per cent perspiration.*
**Thomas Edison**

# 9

# Shenton Park Rehabilitation Campus – Part 1

*If you don't have hope for the future,
you have no power in the present.*

**John Maxwell**

I stayed in the MTW of Royal Perth Hospital until Monday 24 November 2008, when I was transferred to the Shenton Park Rehabilitation Campus (SPRC), three weeks earlier than expected. Word had begun spreading through the medical staff that I was due to go there soon, but I had no idea what they were talking about or what this place was. It was only when people visiting me knew about the facility that they got me excited, as they knew that the medical side of things was coming to an end and the rehabilitation process could begin.

Moving day arrived without me even knowing it and it was rather surreal as it unfolded. Richard and Leanne Ford were visiting, as well as my flat mate Allison, who asked if I knew when I would be going there. The reply was that it should be in a few days time, but that was more likely to be weeks than days. Suddenly, a nurse walked in and said I was being transferred at 11:00 a.m. Allison looked at me as if I had been lying to her, but the shock on my face told her that I was just as surprised as she was.

A quick call to Purds who was due to visit me later in the day, had the removal team assembled, including her son Aidan and they began packing up my things and putting them in the cars, to take across to Shenton Park. After 6 weeks in hospital, my room had almost become my bedroom, with more and more items arriving in the form of gifts and cards, as well as things from home

## A Long Ride Back

that I needed, or would help with my daily living.

So my room was packed up and everything was gone, as we expected the patient delivery system to be on schedule. I was left lying in the room, all alone, waiting for the transfer. The only thing I had was my phone, I think. This was another of the instances, when what we thought was happening at a specific time was not even close to what actually occurred. All perfectly understandable in the public health system with so much to organise, but very frustrating for those not used to how these things worked. The end result was Allison and Purds waiting at Shenton Park all day, while I waited at RPH until around 4:30 p.m. when I was finally transferred. I should mention here that Allison had arrived back from her United Kingdom holiday the day before and her first visit to me resulted in having to help move all of my stuff. She was not very impressed!

I arrived at SPRC around 5:00 p.m. and was moved into a room with a couple of other guys. A few days later, I was shifted to another room, which I was not happy about, but looking back I don't really remember why. An uncomfortable situation with this room occurred when the guy next to me and his female friend were 'catching up' behind the curtain. With nowhere to go and no headphones to put on, I just had to lie there and listen to the squeaky bed. Fortunately it didn't last very long! Changing rooms the next day turned out to be for the best in other ways too, as the patients I would share the room with over the next month or so, quickly became my partners in crime for practical jokes, fun and games with everyone on the Ward, knowing about the shenanigans of the boys in Room H, Ward 10.

In the rush to transfer me from RPH, the hypo granulating cream for my skin grafts was not included, so we were unable to change the dressings that day. No one knew exactly what this cream was called and when they did find out; there was none in stock at the pharmacy. Unbelievably frustrating that a hospital didn't have what a patient needed, but this was all sorted the next day and wasn't really a big deal in scheme of things.

# Shenton Park Rehabilitation Campus – Part 1

The first guy I remember was a teenager named Kevin, who had to have an abscess removed from his testicle. Ouch! He was a bit of a whinger and didn't hang around long, luckily. Martin Haak was in the bed next to mine and had a car accident on his way to the dentist. Martin woke up in hospital, not remembering a thing, with no recollection of what had happened. He looked down at all the bandages and stuff, rang for a nurse and said 'shit, what's the dentist done to me?' Kevin was replaced by Wayne Giles, a rough looking biker with his beard and shaven head who looked and talked really tough – until his wife Sheryl and daughters Rylee, Maddy and Kelsey arrived to visit. They soon had him wrapped around their fingers though! Wayne was on his motorbike with one of his daughters when a car didn't see them and pulled out, sending them both over the handle bars airborne, with Wayne ending up under a truck as well! It wasn't as big as my one though!

The other short stay patients were mostly car or motorbike accident victims. Another long term patient was a young kid named Liam, who took the bed next to Wayne and opposite Martin and me. Liam had been drinking all day with his father, who then decided that he was alright to drive. Obviously Liam believed him, so he got in the car with him. His Dad misjudged a corner, lost control and wrapped their car around a tree. While his Dad was okay (as is often the case) Liam lost a tooth, broke an arm, a leg and his tailbone, among other injuries. Liam was also a bit of a girl's blouse and he became a good target for Wayne, Martin and I to tease and give mild abuse to, with some underlying annoyance that he was here through his own stupidity, but the rest of us simply had accidents. He became the only adult I know who was asking Santa for a front tooth for Christmas! Liam had a very attractive young female doctor who would visit regularly, much to the delight of the other three amigos in the room and we used to tease him about this as well, of course. We all got on really well, but there was one occasion when I realised that Liam was progressing better than everybody thought. I'm not sure if Wayne and Martin were still there or not. Liam was putting a DVD into his portable machine, when he dropped it and it fell on the floor. Instantly he called for the nurse to pick it up for him, which is what most of us had to do anyway. But as he tried again, he clumsily dropped it once more. He was too embarrassed to call for help this time, so he just reached down and picked it up himself. The look I shot at him, along with a couple of choice words reminded Liam that what he did was definitely not cool and it was in his best interests to only call for a nurse when he couldn't do things for himself. Seeing him take advantage of the help we were getting really annoyed me and I made sure he knew it.

At some point during my stay at either RPH, or here in SPRC, I was given a few tools that would become very useful, while I was confined to a bed. The first was a gift from Belinda's holiday to Broome. It was a toy crocodile head on the end of a stick, with a trigger mechanism which opened its mouth when squeezed. It sounds very silly and childish, and it is, but was actually very useful when reaching for things like a pen, headphones etc. A backscratcher would prove to be a lifesaver as well, so that I could reach the areas that really annoyed me. The last tool was the OT stick, which I saw Martin using and demanded from the Occupational Therapy Department. Sam was the OT 'Pocket Rocket' who was the lady to see, when you needed something. She stood about 5'4" and looked too sweet and innocent to carry any authority but when it came to organisation, she was brilliant! The OT stick was simply a piece of dowel, about 60 cm long and about 1 ½ cm wide, which had a hook in one end and a rubber thimble stapled to the other. It was surprising how much I could reach, pull or grab with this thing, particularly the curtain when wanting it opened or closed. This was the best thing ever and such a simple device too. It really was a lifesaver on more than one occasion.

SPRC is an old, shabby looking complex desperately in need of a facelift and décor upgrade. The plain beige and cream interior was very unappealing and added to the mood of people who felt like they were stuck there with no sign of leaving. Despite the shoddy appearances, the work that goes on inside the walls is absolutely brilliant. This is the place to get rehabilitated, rested and recovered while preparing for the transition back to whatever form of normal-

## Shenton Park Rehabilitation Campus – Part 1

ity the patient is heading to. It is a wide open complex, with long concrete pathways joining all of the buildings, but is a bit like a rabbit warren and quite hard to find specific places sometimes. Ward 10, where I was located, was more like the typical hospital Ward, with Room H having a large double door emergency access, which was useful for us to see who was coming and going.

Like all hospitals and caring facilities, the staff were predominately compassionate and thoughtful, even though there seemed to be a lot of foreign nurses and trainee nurses, fresh out of college. They were often the ones we would pick on for practical jokes. A common favourite of mine was when the nurse had to pinch my toes to ensure I still had feeling, after lying down for so long. They would begin by gently squeezing the toes and asking if I could feel it. This was easy to bluff to begin with and respond with a no. It took more concentration when the squeeze would be slightly harder, and the look of panic came across their face when told that I still couldn't feel anything. Finally, they would reach for something to prick my toes with, but usually I or the other patients watching would ruin the fun by bursting out laughing. The nurses were never impressed initially, but always saw the funny side, not long afterward.

Even though I was transferred to SPRC, I still wasn't ready for any rehabilitation. My condition hadn't changed that much and I had to wait the appropriate length of time on traction, before it could be removed and I would be reassessed.

The frustration of dealing with so many different medical personnel and the new staff looking after me was highlighted shortly after I arrived. When I first met the Orthopaedic doctor, he told me that I would be in traction for another 2½ - 3 weeks and won't be going anywhere until at least then. When I questioned that this would be longer than I was first told, he replied by trying to remind me that I had only been in traction for 10 days. I knew it had been longer than that, but without any proof, he wasn't listening. I still had to remain at 30 degrees, so it was simply just lie back and wait - again. An annoying thing with this was that I actually started doubting myself and how long it had been. I knew I was high as a kite most days, but was sure I had the length of time fairly close.

As the dose of drugs wore off that day, the frustration increased as I began to realise that I was still stuck in a bed indefinitely and wasn't able to move very much, or do anything really. The majority of the time I had visitors to occupy me; movies to watch or books to read and was often on the internet, sending emails, so it was only a few times when I wondered how long I would have to go on like this. However, after being in bed for so long, doing the same things became just as boring. Eventually I got sick of reading, sick of watching movies, sick of playing games on the computer, and sick of being in bed. I wanted to get out of bed and I wanted to go home, but as long as I was in bed, I had to keep my brain active and do something! The focus became getting through the days until I was strong enough to stand up.

The next morning, my Orthopaedic doctor came back to say that he thinks I have been in traction longer than 10 days and I may have been right all along. Hmm, funny that! Any decisions about changing my traction condition had to go through Gavin Clark, who wasn't based at SPRC, and was not always available. Until he said so, nothing was going to change. This waiting and not knowing was probably the hardest part at the current time and it seemed that everyone I spoke to had their own opinion of what was happening to me, but nothing they could say for certain.

Finally, on Monday 01 December, the doctors came in and said they would take the traction off. Today was like Christmas for me and I was the happiest I had been in ages! This was actual progress after a month and a half of having to stay in bed. Finally, I could get up and start doing things. I'd be out of bed by the afternoon I thought. Once I was out of traction, I needed to begin sitting up gradually and working my way up to 90 degrees. The traction bag was removed shortly after, but I wasn't going anywhere yet. Slowly, within the next 24 hours, the rehabilitation began. The Orthopaedic doctors had seen my x-rays and were confident that my left leg was not going to drop down any further than it had. This was now

# Shenton Park Rehabilitation Campus – Part 1

about 1 ½ cm shorter than my right leg, which would bring a range of issues later on, when I got back to walking around.

I now had to work my way up to sitting at a 90 degree angle, which was a long, slow, up and down process, as doing it too quickly, would make me dizzy and cause me to nearly pass out. So I would have to lie back down and rest for a while, before trying again. Over the next few days I succeeded in reaching 90 degrees and even attempted to stand a couple of times, with the physiotherapist's help, of course. I was soon sitting up, rejoicing in the fact that this was finally how I could do things again. There was no real success in standing however, as my right heel was the only part of my feet that I could put weight on and this was simply not strong enough to support me yet.

The next challenge was to get onto a commode chair, so I could use the bathroom by myself. With a little help from the physiotherapist and a nurse, I was on it straight away. I still had to be pushed to the bathroom on that occasion, but that was fine by me. Then it was back to bed for a rest, as all that activity had wiped me out. Any commode or wheel chair I used had to have a leg extension to support my leg which was stuck straight. Without this, I wasn't strong enough to hold it up, so it would drop and try to bend itself, which it couldn't, so it felt like it was going to break every time it wasn't held.

It was great timing on Thursday 04 December when Alex and Allison came to visit, bringing me McDonalds for lunch, as my reward for getting out of traction. Sam, from the OT Department brought in a wheelchair and with some help, I was soon sitting in it and feeling like a king on his throne. I required assistance to push me around still, but that didn't last long. So the next few days were spent getting in and out of the wheel chair and sitting in it for long periods to prepare for my upcoming secret mission – getting a day release to go to Busselton and watch the Ironman for a few hours.

This last week had been Ironman training of a different kind, that's for sure and there wasn't much of a taper before race day!

## A Long Ride Back

With the sudden change in activity as rehabilitation started, even the task of transferring from my bed to the wheelchair and back was massively exhausting. It was hard to believe it wasn't that long ago that I could do so much more and still have energy afterwards.

Getting to Busselton to my watch my friends compete was one of my main goals from very early on. With the traction on my leg, I had no chance. Once it came off, I was an 80% chance, but had to show the physiotherapist and OT that I could do all of the things they required and they had to then convince the doctors that I wasn't a risk to myself.

December quickly became a month of milestones, in the lead up to the Ironman:

Monday December 01, I was taken off traction.

Tuesday December 02, I sat up to 90 degrees.

Wednesday December 03, I was back to Royal Perth Hospital to see the Plastic Surgeons, so they could make sure my wounds were healing satisfactorily.

Thursday December 04, I stood up for the first time, since the day of the accident, on 14 October 2008. I also managed to move onto and sit on a commode. I then used a real toilet for the first time since this date as well. I finally managed to move onto and sit in my wheelchair.

Friday December 05, I managed to get from a wheelchair into a car and out again, with help from other people of course.

Saturday December 06, was my Mum's birthday and making this much progress so soon, was also completed with her in mind. I still couldn't walk, but this was good enough for now. Having all my immediate family so far away was really, really hard on some occasions. Being able to do these things, as a token present for Mum was great, even if she wasn't there to see it.

Sunday December 07, was the day of IMWA in Busselton – Would

Shenton Park Rehabilitation Campus – Part 1

I actually achieve the goal I had been dreaming about for two months?

*Genius is the ability to reduce the complicated, to the simple.*
C. W. Cernan

# 10

# The Great Escape

*Just do it!*
**Nike**

During my recovery, Ross and I often talked about Ironman Western Australia and how awesome it would be to see it. While I was in traction, this was never going to happen. As soon as the traction bag was removed, we started planning the trip to Busselton.

On Thursday 04 and Friday 05 December, when I was proving to the physiotherapist and OT that I was well enough to go, the last task was to show them I could get in and out of the car, from the wheelchair, with assistance. I rang Ross and told him that unless I could do that, I could not go. He arrived about two hours later and within half an hour, we had satisfied the powers that be that we could do it. The task itself wasn't really that hard, as the wheelchair had removable arm rests and foot rests and we could get right in close to the back seat. Then, using the handle above the door, I just swung myself across to get some of my bottom on the seat. From there it was a matter of sliding across the seat, to the other side, sitting with my left leg lying straight across the back seat. I had to sit with my back against the door, in this position, with pillows all around me for comfort. Not that hard really, just exhausting.

None of the medical staff were happy for me to go to Busselton, but slowly began to understand how much it meant to me. Of course, they were only worried about me, but I was determined to prove that I would be all right. They had the final say about it, but accepted that if there was any task that they wanted me to do, I wanted the opportunity to try and do it. If I couldn't do it to a point where they were satisfied, then I wouldn't go and that would be fine, but I wasn't going to give up without trying.

Sunday morning arrived and it was an early breakfast for me, with a quick wash in bed and then pack the things required for my big day out. Drugs; of course, phone; hat; sunglasses and water were the priority. Ross wheeled me out to the car, with one of the nurses and we loaded me in. As Ross folded up the wheelchair to place in the boot, we discovered that it wouldn't fit. The one given to me had the ability to tilt backward, so that my back took most of the weight, as opposed to my bottom, which made it a bit larger than normal. This was a great idea, but we couldn't make use of it. So we had to take a standard chair, which was not as comfortable, but still did the job. All loaded up with pillows, blankets, medication, pee bottle and water, we hit the road. Our first stop was McDonalds for breakfast!

We arrived in Busselton, around 10:00 a.m. just in time to see most of the local athletes heading out for their third and final lap of the ride. Peta had swum for a team in the Ironman and met us on our arrival. We would see her teammate Val Best ride past on her bike, shortly afterward. A couple of the guys I knew who were watching with us, gladly offered to help me get from the car to the chair. This was something I knew I could rely on, but was one example of a reason why the doctors were hesitant. I was basically telling them that I had a support team down there that would take care of me like they couldn't imagine. Anything I needed, they would do. So between Ross and Chris Colgate, I was out of the car and into the wheelchair, without having to lift a finger hardly. My friends would ensure that I didn't go back in any worse condition than when I left Perth.

All covered up to protect me from the sun and surrounded by about 10 'surrogate mothers' to keep me fed, hydrated and shaded, we watched from outside the Higgins home for a while as most of the Busselton athletes went past, many as excited to see me as I was to be there.

# The Great Escape

Jenny had set up a shaded area out the front of their place, along with a banana lounge for me to sit on, so my straight leg would be comfortable, if I wanted a break from the wheelchair. Again, just small things that were done, but really nice gestures to ensure I was as comfortable and protected as possible.

We then moved down to the Aid Station further down the road to watch the run. I wanted to get closer to the road to be near the athletes as they ran past, but no one would let me. I had to remain under the shade of a tree, out of the sun, which was very annoying. I knew it was for my own good, but I desperately wanted to be more involved, not just watching. I felt like the kid in the lolly shop who could look but not touch, adding to my frustration.

The first runner I saw was Steve Anstee, who was participating in a team, with Ben Bray swimming and Roy McGregor cycling. These three named themselves 'In It To Win It' and did just that to the teams' event. Three very fast individual times saw them cross the finish line in a blistering 08:47:03. Everyone was yelling at Steve as he ran past us. This point was only a few kilometres from the finish of each lap and we were all going crazy. I yelled out a big 'Come on Fabio', Steve's nickname and he turned, recognising my voice, for a quick glance. He couldn't believe I had made it to watch and he was stoked. He runs like a gazelle most of the time, but after that, he went even quicker.

We stayed there for the rest of the morning and saw most of the Busselton crew each lap – Connie, Max, Michael, Louise, Alex, Gary, Wendy, and Melina Townsend, who was running in Peta's team and most of the others I knew. It was even better when they saw me there and got that extra burst of excitement and energy. For me, it was exciting, frustrating, humbling and fantastic, all at the same time. It was a cloudless blue sky day, in the high 30's, so sitting and watching even in the shade had me sweating like a pig. The blankets and towels covering me to keep me out of the sun didn't help this either, but protection from the sun was of massive importance, particularly for my freshly skin grafted legs.

## A Long Ride Back

Several weeks before race day, Darryl McGrath had come to visit me in Shenton Park and we discussed his preparation for the upcoming Ironman. I'm not sure whose idea it was, but for his next visit, I arranged to get the small soft toy of 'Shaggy' the Scooby Doo character, which had been given to me years ago, brought in to me. Shaggy had been my nickname around town for some time and was often how people referred to me. Darryl picked it up the next time he visited and tied it to his bike for the 180 km ride of the Ironman, as a tribute to me and a reminder that the pain he was suffering wasn't really that bad. Darryl managed to earn a personal best time on the day and I was glad to have given him some inspiration during his race.

It was tremendous to see as many of my friends as I did – either competing, or just hanging out. I wish I could have stayed there longer, but I was grateful for the time I had. Because it was a secret mission, I wanted it to be a surprise; particularly for the athletes I knew competing and I didn't want to distract them from their race day preparation. I should have told more people, as I'm sure many would have made the effort to come over and see me. Katie Greenfield was working in the Massage Tent during the day and was just one of the locals who were disappointed to hear that I was in town, but didn't get to see me.

At around 2:30 p.m. Ross returned to pick me up and I was loaded back into the car. Again, between him and Simon Green, I didn't have to do too much there either. My day was over and we started driving back to Perth. Not long into the return trip, I began to feel really nauseous and called for Ross to pull over. Being propped up against the back door was very handy, as I just opened it up, turned my head and let go everything I had eaten that day. I'm not sure what was going on there, but it was all better out than in, apparently.

The final stop before Shenton Park was KFC for dinner! Then it was back to the Ward and into bed, telling everyone about my day and still buzzing that Ross and I had achieved the goal. It really exhausted me but I knew I would have regretted not doing all I

## The Great Escape

could, to try to get there, especially if I was off traction.

The next day, I slept. And slept and slept. Then I slept some more. I was stuffed! Having Ross bring me down to Busselton to watch my friends do what I couldn't, was simply fabulous, even if it did annoy a lot of doctors and nurses who said I wouldn't be able to handle it and shouldn't go. Being my Coach, Ross understood exactly what that meant to me and he was determined to assist in making it happen. This was the best kind of therapy and came at exactly the right time.

> *Desire is the key to motivation, but it's the determination and commitment to an unrelenting pursuit of your goal –*
> *a commitment to excellence – that will enable*
> *you to attain the success you seek.*
> **Mario Andretti**

# 11

# Shenton Park Rehabilitation Campus – Part 2

*The future depends on what we do in the present.*
*Mahatma Ghandi*

Now that I was off traction and had recovered from the excitement of my escape, it was now time to begin a structured physiotherapy routine and gym work to get as strong as possible, ready for my release sooner, rather than later, all going well. My aim now was to get through the days until I could go home.

On Monday 08 December, I had more x-rays of my pelvis, hip and foot. The next day my doctor advised that I could now weight bare fully on my right leg. This opened the door for me to use crutches, but I had to start with a walking frame first.

Later, that Tuesday afternoon, Russell, the Physiotherapy Supervisor, was back for another session. With the four wheeled pulpit frame, I was able to stand, then hop (as I could only use one foot) from my bed, out of our room's doorway, turn around and hop back, even pausing while the nurses finished changing the bed linen. This went all right and I was soon safely sitting back down on my bed. I was however, absolutely wrecked! While triathlon training, I had run 10 km and felt better than I did doing 5-10 minutes of exercise on this day. My legs, arms and shoulders were all aching. This was not a feeling I liked and for a while I couldn't understand why it was so hard.

The reality of lying around, doing nothing was emphasised during the same session, when Russell told me to flex my calf muscles

## A Long Ride Back

before standing, to get the blood pumping through to the feet. As I looked down, I noticed I didn't have calf muscles anymore! What was once the envy of the ladies who would ride behind me, perving at my backside and legs were now nothing more than loose, flabby skin. They were gone and would need a lot of work to get them back to anything like they were.

I was having two physiotherapy sessions a day in the hope of making a faster recovery and improvement. Weeks of lying down, unable to move were over and it was now time to start getting fit again. The wounds on my legs hadn't healed enough to allow me into the hydrotherapy pool, so it would all have to be done in the gym. My leg muscles were non-existent and because my left leg had been in traction for so long, it did not bend at all. So when I moved, I had to slide my leg sideways or forwards, as I had no quadricep muscle to use to lift it.

The coming weekend was the Busselton Cycle Club's end of year function and I made enquiries about whether I could get down to Busselton again to attend this as well. As you can imagine, one trip was enough, so that idea went quickly out the window. Since it began in 2006, The BCC had given awards out to people for a variety of reasons – Most Improved Male and Female Riders, King of the Mountain, Rising Star, to name a few, as well as some humorous ones, which included The Gravel Rash Award, given to the rider with the worst crash of the year. Naturally I was this year's recipient, so I asked Michael to accept it and say a few words on my behalf. Michael was more than happy to do so and when he mentioned to those gathered that he had a personal update from me, he soon had everyone's undivided attention.

Here I was able to thank everyone for their support and relay my excitement of seeing the Ironman the week before and detail the progress I had made during the week as the rehabilitation began. I also asked that the winner of next year's Gravel Rash Award, do something that was not a serious accident and definitely didn't involve any trucks! There were not too many dry eyes during our speech. I had chosen Michael to speak for me, as he was the 2007

# Shenton Park Rehabilitation Campus – Part 2

winner and knew what this humorous but meaningful award acknowledged. My thoughts were of desperately wanting to be there, having fun and seeing my friends again, while theirs was to have me taking part and helping with the presentations, like I usually do. Leaving Andy Milne alone to do this was definitely not what he wanted, but he would pay me back in a few months' time.

The week of 15-18 December 2008 was when I made the most progress standing up. The pulpit frame was changed to Granny's Zimmer frame to get me over to the parallel bars in the physiotherapy gym. It took more than a few laps to get my confidence up as I was constantly paranoid of falling. My cardio fitness was obviously non-existent and I was soon keeled over, sucking in the big breaths. Then it was off to the couch to do leg stretches, to increase the flexibility in my left leg, which didn't bend at all, after being dislocated and then held straight for so long. I had been working on this every day and within a week had progressed from zero bend to about 40 degrees. Standing up and sitting down was still a bit dodgy sometimes, as I didn't have the confidence or strength in my legs to support me.

I was making good progress with my mobility, but the skin grafts were still restricting other things. The next goal to aim for was being able to have a shower by myself. Having one or two nurses in there with me was fun sometimes, but mostly it was just weird and awkward.

Once I was able to shower regularly, still using the shower trolley though, having a nurse accompany me got a little easier to deal with, especially as most of them were mature ladies, so it was a bit like having your Mum in there with you. Not really cool, but tolerable if it had to be. As my wounds progressed and I began to get more mobility, I was able to do most of the showering and eventual dressing changes on my wounds, myself.

The biggest bonus to this was that I could remove the bandages at my own pace and control the pain I felt, as opposed to having a nurse do it and ripping it off, along with any new skin that had been trying to grow. Towards the end of my stay, I was doing nearly everything myself, only requiring help to wrap my legs once any relevant cream was applied to the areas I had missed or couldn't reach. This was great for my independence, especially when I couldn't walk properly yet, and was just beginning to use a wheelchair.

There is a saying that if you have to do something you don't like, then you should rip it off like a band-aid, because then it will hurt less and only for a short amount of time. This was an expression I have really come to dislike, as ripping any bandage off my leg, would remove several layers of skin in the process. These were layers that the surgeons had just put on and that my body was slowly reproducing. Needless to say whenever I hear that saying, I just cringe, as I'm reminded of the damage that could be done by doing just that. When it came to removing bandages and dressings, I wanted to be the one in control and it was done slowly and carefully and I didn't care how long it took. I was also going to make sure it didn't hurt very much at all.

As far back through my life as I can remember, most of my friends have been female. Sure, I had my close guy mates, but the ratio was always more ladies than men. This continued throughout my life, even when I moved from New Zealand to Australia. There were never many girlfriends who eventuated from this great ratio, unfortunately, but having them around was always good fun. This ratio would work to my advantage, particularly here at SPRC, as on more than one occasion, others would comment on how many ladies I had visiting me. And of course, this was noticed more by the males I had around me.

Most of the roommates I had at either RPH or SPRC could not believe how many good looking women I knew and how this continuous stream of female visitors never seemed to end. When I mentioned that most of them lived in Busselton, they would tell me that they would be moving there when they got out of hospital. On the occasions when several ladies would visit around the same time, the looks on the other guys' faces were priceless, but it was good to see them smiling as well. I, of course, would play on this, when I

# Shenton Park Rehabilitation Campus – Part 2

knew who was expected to visit during the day.

On a couple of occasions at SPRC, I would have to go for a shower or to the gym for physiotherapy and would often know that visitors were expected. So I would say to the other guys in the room – 'If a gorgeous looking blonde / brunette, about 5' 4' or 5' 7' comes in to visit, then tell her I'll be back soon'. I would then return to find them all chatting together and the amazed looks on their faces was worth a thousand words as they realised I was right and not just talking shit. They were very happy to have me as a roommate and were definitely not complaining about the quality of visitors I was producing.

On Thursday 18 December, I was just about to be taken to the gym for another session, when Julie Bray and her sons Ben and Louis arrived to visit. They kindly offered to take me there and watched while I did the exercises. This day was one of the first days where I was attempting to walk again. Now, I don't mean this to sound like I was ever in danger of not being able to walk, but it was training the muscles to remember how to redo the motion of walking, so they would do the process automatically in the future. The exercises involved walking (or in my case shuffling) between parallel bars, back and forth for about 5 minutes. I don't think Ben and Louis had ever seen real therapy before and were taking in the seriousness of the situation, even though they were both only teenagers. Ben offered to video record footage of the session for me, as I was already taking photos throughout my recovery.

The next morning, I was back to RPH for an inspection of my skin grafts and a dressing change. There were a couple of areas, where my leg joined my torso, which were not healing, as the skin here was always moving and stretching as I became more mobile. Without one person dedicated to looking after me regularly, this area couldn't be monitored properly. The hardest part here was that the progress of standing and walking was stretching and tearing the skin that was trying to heal. I was in a catch 22 position and would be for some time!

## A Long Ride Back

This Friday was also the first day that I was allowed out on day leave for a few hours, since my day trip to Busselton. When I got back from RPH, Michael, Ben and Louis were waiting to visit, as they were in town for the State Swimming Trials. The look on Michael's face was priceless, when I asked him if I could join them for dinner. Disbelief, followed by amazement, excitement and a yes, of course. So Michael, Ben and Louis loaded me into the car and packed up the wheelchair. We headed to the only upstairs restaurant, that Michael knew, which had an elevator. Jimmy Deans, at Scarborough Beach, in Perth.

When we got there, we discovered that the lift was out of order! What are the odds! However, there was access from the car park around the corner, up the hill, so after a bit of solid pushing from Ben, I was soon up and checking out the menu. A massive burger with the works and fries was soon being devoured and I was content for a little while. I declined Michael's joking offer of a beer, on this occasion, as I couldn't go back to SPRC half cut! This was one of the highlights of my SPRC stay and was a fantastic evening out with a great family, even though Julie was back at home.

This occasion was possible, mostly because I had the confidence of being with these three guys who could handle looking after a very unbalanced patient and this was very reassuring. Even though I was apprehensive about being outside of SPRC and away from the safety of the medical staff, I had complete confidence that Michael and his boys would take excellent care of me.

The Brays returned the next morning to pick me up again and take me to Challenge Stadium for their swim meet so I could see the boys' race. Personal bests for both of them, so we were all pleased.

When I got back on Saturday afternoon, Brad and Purds, with three of their boys Josh, Sam and Aidan called in to say hello. When they left, I closed my eyes for a little rest and woke 4 ½ hours later! The outdoor activities of the past 24 hours had exhausted me, but it was well worth it.

Christmas was fast approaching and the excitement around the

## Shenton Park Rehabilitation Campus – Part 2

Ward was growing as any patients who were allowed, aimed to get released in time or planned day trips home. I had been invited to spend Christmas Day with Allison and her family in Perth. Being able to get around in a wheelchair was very convenient and it was another big day out, with her cousins, uncles and aunties, and Santa of course. I had already met some of them before, but was welcomed into their family gathering like I was one of them, which was very special. Boxing Day was a chance for me to rest and recover from my Christmas Day celebrations. Max and Jenny visited the following day and took me out to Cottesloe Beach for lunch. Any chance I got to leave the bed, the room, the Ward or the whole facility was taken as often as I could, from now on.

Two of my roommates had managed to check themselves out before Christmas, which was good for them, but brought the hilarious antics of Room H to a dramatic halt. Martin was the first to go and after the trouble he had with his wrist getting infected hours before his last attempt, it was pleasing to see a successful result. Martin was replaced by Phil, who could only be described as 'a grumpy old man'. Wayne was next and how quiet the evenings became without his girls coming to see him. It quickly became far too quiet and very, very boring! Liam had an overnight visit and was back Boxing Day, before being discharged in time for New Years. A funny experience that happened with Liam at the start of December was when he received a Hannah Montana Advent Calendar in the lead up to Christmas, as they were the only type left at the shop. Martin, Wayne and I gave him so much shit about it, that a few days later, his Mum brought us in one each. That shut us up - for about 5 minutes!

On Tuesday 30 December, I was able to try the Continuous Passive Motion (CPM) machine to assist with my leg bend. This was a big, bulky contraption, which was wheeled into my room and set up on my bed. My left leg was strapped to it and the apparatus was turned on. The machine moved back and forth, slowly raising my knee up and then straightening it out again. Very little bend was achieved here, but it was progress nonetheless. This machine forced my leg to bend more than I could physically make it, so it

## A Long Ride Back

was a painful process, but necessary. The best thing with this was that because I could control how fast and how much it moved, I could do a hard session and really force the leg to bend and then ease it off for a second session and have it bending only a little bit. This second run usually resulted in me drifting off to sleep while the machine did the work for me.

New Year's Eve came and went with nothing exciting to share. No visitors, funnily enough, so it was just hanging out in bed after cruising around in the wheelchair, or going for a short walk with the crutches.

As my skin was healing more each day, it became time to wear Second Skins, which are a stretchy, compression material worn as clothing, which helps the skin grow and repair while minimising scarring, most of the time. They are common with burns victims' recovery. These were very tight fitting and took a lot of getting used to as I wasn't able to put them on by myself. I would end up wearing them every day for the next 6 months.

Once I was allowed out of bed and had begun going through the walking process, wearing clothes was another issue I had to deal with. Being in bed was never a problem and often I could just wear a T-shirt most of the time, if that. The hospital gowns were convenient because they could be put on and taken off easily, but they had to be buttoned up at the back and even when done so, were still not a great solution. Jo Wilson came to the rescue one day, when she smuggled one home and made some alterations to it for me. Adding a strip of Velcro down the back instead of the buttons meant I could turn it around and wear it more like a shirt. It hung low enough to cover things up, so I didn't have my bare arse on display, not to mention my injuries. The Velcro was much easier to do up, rather than having to fiddle around with the buttons, especially when trying to balance, and use crutches etc. It only sounds like a small problem, but it did make one inconvenient thing, much less of a hassle. Unfortunately, in the rush to leave Shenton Park, her handy work was left behind. I hope that someone else is using it now and it is serving a purpose for them, just as it did for me!

# Shenton Park Rehabilitation Campus – Part 2

My first Plastic Surgery dressing inspection of the year was Friday 02 January 2009. This was the day I got to ask them all the important questions about going home. I hadn't bothered before now, as until Orthopaedics had given the bone structures the all clear, there was no point in worrying about my release. Plastics were keen to let me go and were organising follow up care in Busselton. The Orthopaedic Doctors were keen too, but would have a meeting on Monday to discuss it with OT and physiotherapy staff.

I was hoping for release around 10 January 2009 to score a lift home with the Busselton swimmers who would be up in Perth for another swim meet. This was Michael's final stint as Coach of The Busselton Swimming Club and although he was unaware of it, he got very close to receiving a phone call to reserve a place for me in the car on the way home. We had semi-joked about it a few weeks back when he was up visiting in mid-December, but neither of us had any idea how close this came to being a reality.

The weekend dragged on and Monday couldn't come fast enough for me. Sleepless nights, nervous tension at having to step out of my comfort zone and head back to reality hit me hard on more than one occasion. With the tremendous support I would have back in Busselton, these thoughts were completely unnecessary, but when you have been in a hospital bed for nearly three months and are learning how to do some of the everyday tasks again, balanced on one and a half legs with crutches, it was more than a little daunting for me. While I couldn't wait to get out of there, my condition was not exactly ideal. I had to put my faith in the doctors, as they did know what they are talking about!

On the Sunday afternoon, a young guy arrived into our room. He was 20-25 years old and had just had his left leg amputated from the knee down after a Motocross jump landing that went pear shaped. He had quite good spirits and made me realise even more, how lucky I was to still have both legs - they just didn't work properly yet. And the key word was yet! Unfortunately he changed Wards, a few days later, so any hope I had of having fun and causing trouble with him, were over. The only other guy left in the room was Phil and he was too deaf to hear me take the piss out of him. That afternoon, I jumped in the wheelchair to do some therapy of my own. To get strong on the bike, we would ride up and down the 3 km of Sues Hill, in Busselton. To strengthen my arms, I wheeled myself up the path to the café and down again. It was a hard, slow slog doing that three times and I'd rather have been doing it on a bike. A few pedestrians were wondering what the hell I was doing. After the third repeat, so was I.

On Monday 05 January I saw the Orthopaedic doctor again, who advised that I could begin weight bearing on my left leg, with 20% of my body weight. I was amazed to find out that he had no idea my left leg had been dislocated in the crash though! More x-rays followed and I was soon weight baring 50% on my left foot. Finally being able to put some decent pressure on this leg, lifted the confidence with things like walking with crutches, using the Zimmer frame and even getting in and out of the wheel chair. With the work I was doing in the gym and using the CPM machine, I had reached a knee bend of around 45 degrees.

As I was preparing to leave SPRC, the nurses discussed my on-going medication, which included the Clexane injections, which had to be continued for a few weeks, even after I was released from hospital until I became more active again. This meant that I had to learn how to inject this myself. Not being a big fan of needles, I was not keen on this idea, but after a few tries, it became a lot easier and was often better than having someone else do it. There is an art to doing this injection, which requires choosing a fatty part of the stomach (plenty of options for me) and pulling the needle out at the right speed and angle, so as not to cause bleeding; lingering, stinging pain and heavy bruising. Not easily done most of the time.

On Tuesday 06 January, Brad and Purds arrived to visit and we headed out to lunch in Mullaloo. As we came back down the corridor, one of the nurses came running out to say that I was being transferred to Busselton Hospital on Thursday 09 January at 7:00 a.m. Not the news I was expecting to hear from her and the result was me bursting into tears as a range of emotions suddenly swept

# Shenton Park Rehabilitation Campus – Part 2

through me. The main thought I had was how I would cope at home, after becoming so dependent on other people for the past 3 months. As much as I wanted to get out of hospital, it had become my comfort zone and I was very apprehensive about leaving. But once the tears dried up, there were smiles all around and we gladly began to pack up most of my stuff for Brad and Purds to take back home for me. With just the bare essentials left behind, the countdown was on to get back to Busselton.

So I was spending my last days at SPRC, writing notes for the final instalment of the latest update to email out, hoping never to return there to stay ever again and also hoping that none of my friends have anything happen to them that would put them in there as well. SPRC is a great facility, with fantastic staff, but you have to hurt yourself pretty badly to earn a stay here. I was really looking forward to being back in Busselton with my own physiotherapist, masseuse, doctor and all my friends of course, to begin doing things for myself once again.

Thursday morning finally arrived and eventually I was loaded into a Patient Transportation Vehicle and driven from Perth to Busselton, strapped onto a stretcher, looking out the back window. It was a very nerve wracking trip, as I was constantly hoping the drivers in the cars following us, were paying attention and weren't going to rear end us, as I was not able to move if we had an accident. Not a place I was comfortable being for a long period of time. The drive from Perth to Busselton, in the van took over 3 hours and I hardly managed to sleep at all due to the vast array of mixed emotions and my apprehensive feelings towards finally coming home.

*The only place success comes before work is in the dictionary.*
***Vidal Sassoon***

# 12

# Home – Finally!

*If you're not giving the world your best,
what world are you saving it for?*
**Ladainian Tomlinson**

The only thing stopping me from going directly home to my house was the paperwork needed to organise getting my leg dressings changed, using home nursing care. Actually leaving hospital could be days or weeks away, but at least in Busselton it would be easier for my visitors to get to me and I could start planning how to try to get my life back on track.

Busselton Hospital is fairly stereotypical of a small country facility with décor that looked like it had been around for the past 20 years. The Main Ward housed all patients, regardless of age, illness or sex and was mostly occupied by elderly people. It seemed that the staff enjoyed having a younger patient to look after and they enjoyed the fact that I could do most things for myself and didn't really need much help from them. Regardless of how any health care facility looks, the important factor is of course ensuring that the majority of the staff are kind; caring; good at and enjoy their job. The appearance of the walls, curtains, and flooring doesn't matter much at all, but when you are in the surrounds for anything more than a few days, often bored senseless and wanting to go home, you start noticing things that need improvement, touch ups and refurbishment.

Allison arrived to help me get set up and Peta came by after she finished work. It was good to be one step closer to being home. We used the week in Busselton Hospital to get things organised for my return to the house. Occupational Therapy inspected my bathroom and arranged for the showerhead to be replaced with a removable hose for me to use. I had to use a chair to sit on when I showered, as I couldn't support myself for too long yet. I required the use of this for several months as it was easier to sit and wash myself, than to try and shower standing up.

The next major goal was to be out of Busselton Hospital before 14 January 2009, as that would be three months since my accident. I was in hospital still, but had some freedom to come and go. The following morning, Aidan picked me up and we drove to Fitzroy Cycles in Bunbury to pick up my damaged bike. It was the first time I had seen it, but surprisingly, it didn't look too bad. The Aero Bars had snapped and the frame had a massive chunk missing, but the rest was mostly just scratches, with a few cracks. Nevertheless, it was a write off and wouldn't be ridden again.

This bike was bought off Neville Sunderland, who had bought it for his son Scott, to try and entice him back from track cycling to road racing. Scott was loving his time on the track and was working his way up after representing Western Australia at National level. From here he went on to ride for the Australian team at the World Championships and would go on to win gold medals at the 2008 Beijing Olympics. The Trek Time Trial bike was the same model that Lance Armstrong rode in the 2004 Tour de France, when riding for the US Postal Service team. The blue and white frame with the red racing stripe was a beautiful bike and although I could never ride it as well as Scott did, I loved being on it.

Kitted out in my blue Busselton Cycle Club gear as well, it almost looked like I knew what I was doing when I rode it. Having such an awesome bike get destroyed like it did was heartbreaking and I couldn't bring myself to get rid of it for over two years. Whatever bike I replaced it with would never be the same and it definitely wouldn't be blue, that's for sure!

On Saturday morning, Allison took me down to The Goose Café, where the local cyclists would meet for coffee after their morning ride. This brought me back to my familiar surroundings and it

## Home – Finally!

was great to sit and chat with my friends again, many of whom nearly fell off their bikes when they finished their ride and saw me! It's okay, they were on the grass and there were no trucks around!

I really only stayed in hospital over the weekend, because I was too scared to go home. I went to the house for a few hours to see how I felt, and became comfortable enough getting around on crutches and testing out the bathroom, toilet and kitchen. It was now time for me to start becoming fully independent once more. Even though I was slowly achieving this, I had been taken care of for nearly 3 months and the thought of having to do things by myself again, was very daunting.

On Monday 12 January 2009, with a day to spare, I left hospital and moved back home. The goal of being home before the 3 month mark was reached and it was great to be back in my own bed, and a lot closer for my friends to visit, instead of being 3 hours away.

Even though I was home, I didn't really do much. My friend Tamlyn Dillon had loaned me her La-Z-Boy chair and I spent a lot of time lying and sleeping in it. At the beginning, I would exhaust myself walking from my bedroom to the lounge – a distance of less than 20 metres – and have to lie down for another rest. I was still on pain killers and other medication, was using crutches to walk around and had daily care from the lovely ladies Rosalie, Jackie and Jan at the Home Nursing Discharge Service who would come and change my dressings each morning.

Another positive of being back at home, was the ability to eat real food. Some of the meals in hospital were delicious and others were absolute crap. But when you are mass producing food for hundreds of people, you can't ask for too much. The worse thing was probably the rotating menu and being in there for nearly 3 months, meant that I had every selection, very regularly. Now that I was home, I could begin putting some serious weight back on, seeing as I only weighed a little over 60 kg still.

Wednesday 14 January 2009 was my first physiotherapy session with Jeff Greenfield from Physio Southwest. I had approximately

50 degrees bend in my left knee and our main focus was increasing this to return as close to normal as possible. The sessions would begin with a heat pack strapped across my knee, followed by Jeff trying to loosen the area around my kneecap. Then I would try to lift my straight leg off the ground and also try to bend it as much as I could. Jeff would then use his elbow for some deep tissue massage which was very painful for me but fun for him! Then I would go out to the stationary bike and do some back and forth cycling motions, pushing one leg until I reached restriction and then the other leg until I reached restriction, as I didn't have enough range of motion to go all the way around. The session lasted for just under an hour, but by the time it was over, I was stuffed. All of my fitness and muscle mass was gone, and the small amounts of exercise I had done at Shenton Park didn't seem to have contributed much. My diary record shows that on Sunday 18 January, I was tired, sore and exhausted with no energy at all.

As physiotherapy continued, I was given a list of exercises to do at home as well, in order to increase my overall strength. To assist this, I bought a set of ankle weights and would wear these around the house as much as possible, as well as doing exercises with them on. They were only 2 kg each, but felt like much more as I struggled to lift my legs off the ground to any height.

Once I was out of hospital and getting around fairly well by myself, the visits from my friends dropped off and it was often me catching up with them for coffees, either at their place or in town, usually after they had been for a ride. Everyone had continued on with their lives and now that I was out of hospital and back at home, normality would soon return and they would see me when I was out and about. I was still feeling quite isolated and even though I was getting my independence back, the drop in attention was quite sudden and I didn't like it.

I often felt that now I was back at home, no one cared about me anymore. This was of course the furtherest thing from the truth, but what a person thinks and feels is very real to them and that was exactly how I felt. I was however in a no win situation. I craved the

# Home – Finally!

attention and caring from my friends, but at the same time, I didn't want to talk about my situation or have to explain how things were going; what the latest news was; or how I was feeling. I quickly became sick of talking about me and even now; I still hate it when people ask how things are going and if I am back riding my bike.

Because my leg had been straight and dormant for so long and had only had a month or so of limited use, it had become nearly impossible to move it without using my arms or other foot, especially when lying or sitting down. Having the luxury of my own sized bed as opposed to the single one in hospital meant that I had the extra space, but was unable to use it. Rolling over took all of my energy and I could not get comfortable enough to sleep for any long periods. I actually returned to having more pain relief at home than I did at the end of my hospital stay, as well as sleeping tablets in an effort to try and get some decent amount of sleep at night. I didn't have the muscle mass in my leg to move it much at all and when the bed covers added their weight, it felt like I had a ton of bricks on top of me. The frustration of being in this situation was again highlighted as I was well and truly on the road of rehabilitation and was back living at home, but my leg was still limiting what I could do.

On Wednesday 21 January, I returned to physiotherapy for more of the same. Jeff was keen to get me making progress as early as possible, so we ditched the crutches and I tried walking. With plenty of aids to reach for along the way, it was a successful mission and a massive turning point to know that I was going to get stronger, faster and head in the direction of back to normal, sort of. My left knee bend had increased to approximately 55 degrees.

By the end of the next week, Friday 30 January, I had about 60 degrees bend and we discussed aiming for 5 degrees every week. This should put me at 180 degrees with full knee bend function, in around 26 weeks, a year at the most. Wow, this time in 2010, I should have full use of my leg and be able to do everything I could before. Some days it seemed like this date was an eternity that was too far away to comprehend and other times it felt as though I would be at that stage a long time before that date. When aiming for 5 degrees of progress per week with Jeff, we had no idea whether this was even achievable, but it was our starting point nonetheless.

Physiotherapy continued usually two or three times per week, each time resulting in mixed emotions. Yes, I could see and feel myself making progress, but at the same time, the results were so minimal that they hardly seemed worthwhile at all, some times. But not once did Jeff ever entertain the thoughts of giving up; feel that things weren't working; or that any result was not worth mentioning, regardless of its size. The support that Jeff showed me mentally, was probably more important than what he did physically, as he understood that it was more about what he said and how I felt, than actual results, particularly this early on, when they were so insignificant. This is something I have always been appreciative of with Jeff, whose professionalism combined with his sense of humour and triathlon experience were the perfect combination to help me at exactly the right time.

As I was getting stronger and more mobile, I was using the crutches more and the wheelchair less. Basically, I hated the chair and felt like I was insulting people who had to be in them every day of their lives. Because my leg couldn't bend, it had to lie straight out in front of me, adding to the unwanted attention being drawn to me and making me feel even more embarrassed. Even though I didn't often 'need' the wheelchair, it did have its uses, mainly for the convenience of getting around, when I knew it was the best option, but didn't want to use it. One such occasion was when Peta and I, Purds and Allison went to see a concert by The Waifs at Leeuwin Estate Winery on Australia Day, in January 2009. The distance from the car park to the grassed area where we were sitting was too far for me to manage, even on crutches. Having a wheelchair eliminated this problem. It was also interesting to see how much respect a wheelchair gives you, as a lot of people would move out of the way or offer help to get through the tricky areas, which was nice.

By mid-February, I was walking without crutches most of the time and hadn't been in the wheelchair since Australia Day. Most

## Home – Finally!

of the time, I was getting around by myself very well. There was even one morning at home, when I got out of bed and walked to the lounge, almost normally. A few hours later, when I awoke from my mid-morning snooze on the La-Z-Boy and needed to go to the bathroom, I looked for the crutches to assist me. I couldn't find them and couldn't work out how I had got from A to B without them. After gingerly exploring the house looking for them, I found them leaning beside my bed, where I had left them the night before. I then came to the conclusion that I obviously didn't really need them much anymore.

I was back around my circle of friends again and becoming more mobile every day. I did not have to rely on other people for rides to and from physiotherapy, or coffee catch-ups any more. So the next thing to organise was of course the 'Thank You Drinks' gathering. This was held on Monday 09 February 2009 at The Busselton Soccer Club, who kindly waived the room hire fee and added to the bar sales in order for us to donate $250.00 to the Royal Flying Doctors Service. This was my chance to thank everyone for all they had done for me over the past four months as well as single out a few individuals for specific mentions. Of course, I was in tears before I had even started and with a few brief glimpses around the room, I definitely wasn't alone. Once my speech was over, I was offered a well done and hand shake from Michael. The end result however, was me bawling my eyes out in a massive bear hug. But it was amazing how much better I felt after doing so.

The first few months of physiotherapy and rehabilitation, despite the progress we were making, were boring and repetitive and felt like Ground Hog day, once again. Eat, physio, sleep, eat, sleep, exercise, eat, and sleep. I was getting increasingly frustrated and there wasn't anything I could do about it. Increasing my exercise and physiotherapy workouts just made me more tired, so I would spend the rest of the day sleeping, as I was exhausted. I was trying to get off the painkillers as well, but sleeping most of the day meant I wasn't tired at night. Sleeping tablets helped, but I was also conscious of getting too used to them. I found myself back in a revolving circle that had no end in sight.

## A Long Ride Back

I had lost about 14 kg within days of being admitted to hospital and the staff were constantly trying to get me to put weight on. I was eating just about everything in front of me, most meals as well as snacking on chocolate and treats in between. I was trying to convince the Nutritionist that once I was home and eating proper food again, the weight would return. Funnily enough, this was exactly what happened and I was up to 65 kg, by mid February 2009 and went on to around 70 kg by May. It was more fat rather than muscle and by the end of the year I was close to 75 kg again, with a sizable belly to match.

In March 2009, Mum and Dad came across from New Zealand, for their first visit since the accident. We had decided early on, that there was no point in them coming over, until I was out of hospital at a point where I could do most things independently. When talking to them, while I was in RPH, they were very keen to come across to Perth straight away. But we decided that the time wasn't right, as there wasn't really anything they could do. The reality of them coming over then, would be having to stay in a hotel; probably organising a rental car; having to pay for meals and other expenses; and visiting me each day, when I was so drugged up that all they would really be doing, is sitting next me and looking at the state I was in. I saw that as an absolute waste of time and money and would just be a very frustrating and annoying time for everyone. There was nothing they could do for me in person, that they couldn't do back home in New Zealand.

Now, don't get me wrong, there were days when I would have loved to have seen my family there beside me, but I was in a stable condition and just needed time to heal and get to a stage where I would be more coherent and responsive.

I didn't want Mum and Dad to have to do everything for me and we all needed to enjoy the time we had while they were here. Their time and energy would be put to better use when I was at home and mobile, instead of bed bound and helpless. The Home Nursing Discharge Service ladies were still coming every day to help change my dressings and make sure I was healing well.

## Home – Finally!

On Thursday 19 March, I returned the crutches and wheelchair to SPRC, before heading to the airport to collect Mum and Dad. Needless to say it was a very emotional reunion at Perth International Airport and they were both surprised at how well I was doing. A few hours later, we were back in Busselton, after talking non-stop the whole way home. The next day, it was time for show and tell, as they saw my injuries first hand and the progress photos. It was good to have explained things first and for them to see the result second, as it helped them to understand things more and not freak out as much.

During their stay, we did a few of the tourist things around the region and I even managed to walk the Jetty when we visited the Underwater Observatory. I was stuffed after that though! Any spare time around the house, Mum and Dad did what they do best – cleaning and tidying inside and outside. Like most parents, there is no such thing as 'don't do that please', or 'just sit down and relax', so it was less hassle to let them potter around and do what they wanted. Mum and Dad also got to meet a few of my fabulous network of friends, when Max and Jenny and Michael and Julie came over for dinner. On a visit to The Goose Café, they met Connie and on another occasion, had lunch with Kym and Sharon. Dinner with Brad and Purds and Allison was a given, of course and her Mum, Glenis was in town, so that was nice as well. They had met Aidan back in 2006, when watching me compete in my first Ironman, and were keen to catch up with him as well. It was good for them to see that I was well looked after and put some faces to the names I had been talking about over the years.

During their stay, Dad asked the question that I'm sure a few people had wondered about. After coming so close to losing my 'tackle', did everything still work properly? He was pleased to hear that they were all fine and in good working order. He's got nine grandchildren from my two sisters and he's worried that I can't contribute to extending the family? I think Mum and Dad have all the grandkids they need, thank you very much! It was however, very reassuring for myself to know that everything was okay.

## A Long Ride Back

Nine days after they arrived, we were back in Perth saying goodbye, but we had planned my trip home for a few months time, so we knew that we would see each other again soon.

After months of rehabilitation, Jeff and I could finally see significant improvement and the sessions continued with more variety as I was given more exercises to do. Soon, I had reached 100 degrees of bend in my left leg. I was going to the gym on the weekends and had begun doing short walks, slowly increasing the distances. I was becoming more mobile and so it was time to think about getting back to work. I returned to my job at Carpet Choice on Wednesday 08 April 2009 and lasted two hours. I carried that on with a few hours a day for the rest of the month.

On Friday 03 April we discovered that I could do full cycling rotations, if I stood up off the seat. This was still sore as it was a very tight flexion, so I could only manage a few of these. But it was a big progression as it meant I could work the knee bend harder as well as achieving a rare psychological accomplishment. I was not far from riding the bike properly again, even it was only standing still. At the session on Monday 20 April, we tried out the stationary bike again. I had about 105 degrees of bend by this stage and could sit on the seat and rotate my legs in a full cycling revolution – just. It was still very tight and painful, but there was just enough stretch to do it.

Every scan or x-ray report I had of my left knee, after the accident, said the same thing - massive bruising on the bone. This was thought to be a reason why it would not bend and it was hoped that once this went away, things would improve. Even scans 12 months later showed the bruising still around, but when it finally faded away, the knee flexion did not improve much past 110 – 120 degrees.

The morning of Friday 24 April, was when I tried my first long run. And by long, I mean massive! I ran from the Busselton Fitness Centre Gym, to the trees on the way towards the Busselton Jetty and back. This was a distance of less than 500 metres return and

# Home – Finally!

when I say run, I really mean slowly shuffle along, not much faster than a very slow walking pace, or a snail on steroids.

Two days later, I tried out the treadmill at Michael's house to see how I would go running on a machine. Much to our surprise, I went all right and we both thought that maybe there would be some amount of running in the future, but no idea of exactly how much.

As the rehabilitation progressed, in my mind I always wanted to be physically stronger than I was before the crash. Sometimes I thought this would be easy, with the amount of work I was doing in physiotherapy and the gym, but I wasn't taking into account how far back I had to start from. With basically no muscle at all on my body, it was worse than the average unfit person who suddenly decides they are going to start working out. They usually have some muscle mass and often have plenty of fat that they can convert. I had nothing. I was skin and bones, with a little bit of a belly, but not much really.

While Mum and Dad were here, we had begun to make plans to return home to New Zealand to see the rest of my family. I wanted them to be reassured that I was basically alright and this gave me the added incentive to keep on with the strenuous rehabilitation program. The donor site on my right buttock was finally beginning to show some solid improvement, but this needed to be fully healed and I needed enough knee bend to be able to go back home without requiring any help with my wound dressings.

*Success is the sum of small efforts repeated day in and day out.*
*Robert Collier*

*The fastest bike in the world…when the right legs are on it!*
*Photo Credit – Steve Crenfeldt*

*All banged up! It doesn't look too bad at first glance, but on closer inspection you could see it wasn't repairable at all.*
*Photo Credit – Steve Crenfeldt*

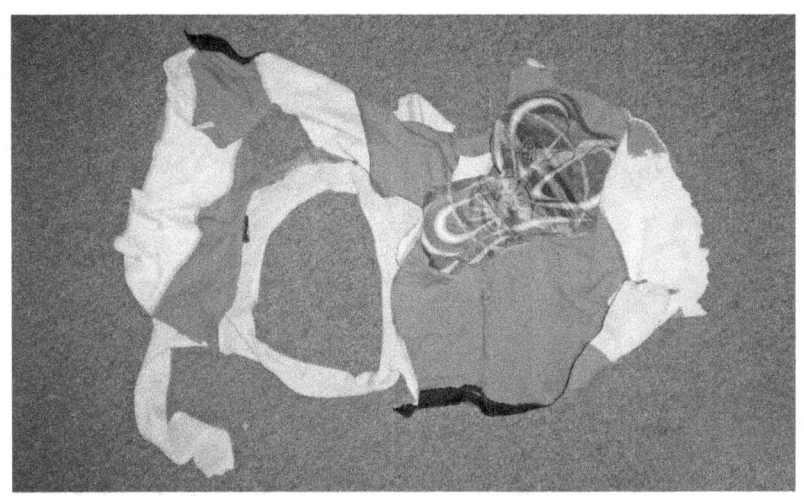

*The remains of my cycling knicks. Not much left of these afterwards.*
*Photo Credit – Steve Crenfeldt*

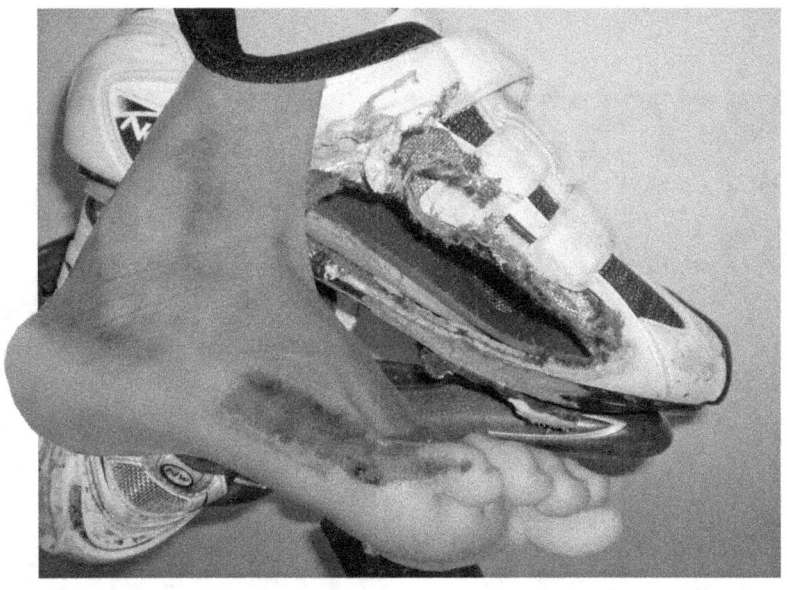

*The comparison of how my shoe and foot looked after the accident. Carbon Fibre shoes, definitely saved my right foot...and my left leg... and me of course!*
*Photo Credit – Steve Crenfeldt and Leonie Paine*

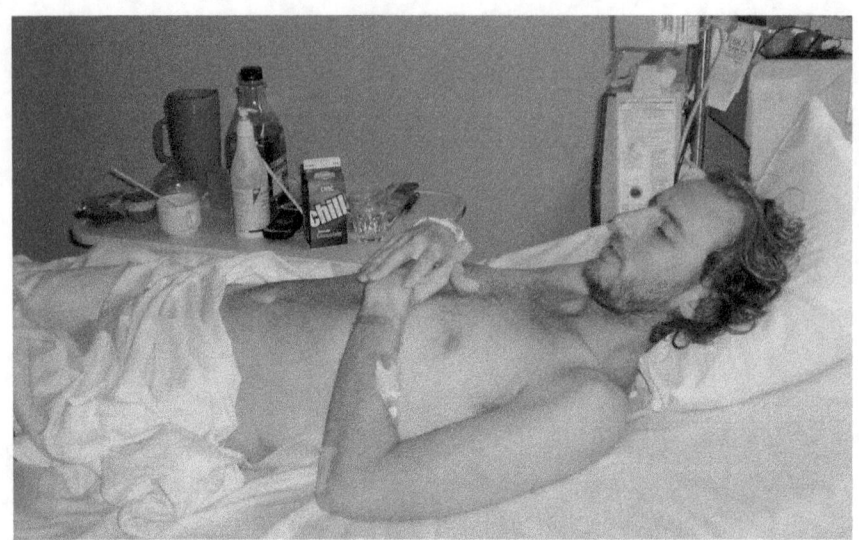

*20 October 2008, nearly one week after the accident. This is what I would be doing for over 2 months.*

*Photo Credit – Allison Slack*

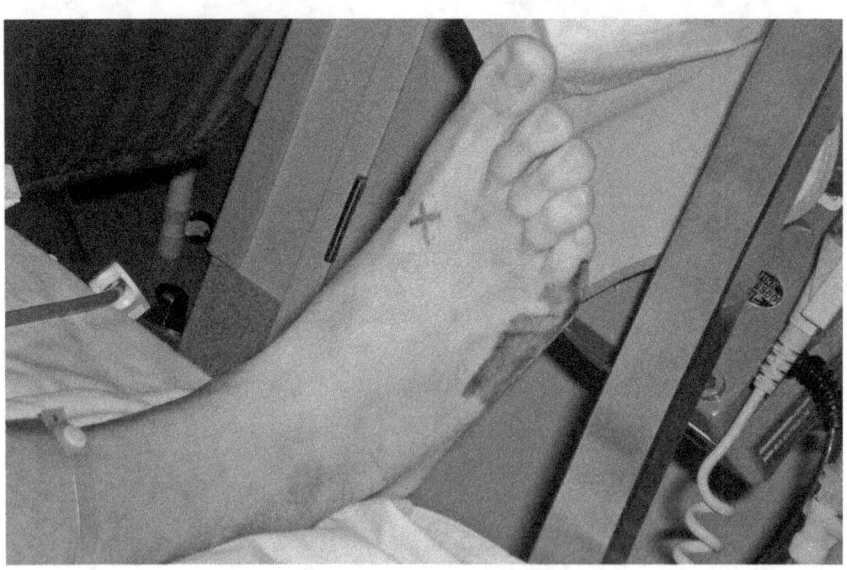

*The bruising slowly leaving my foot. X marks the spot to take my pulse, so the nurses didn't hurt me, when trying to find it.*

*Photo Credit – Allison Slack*

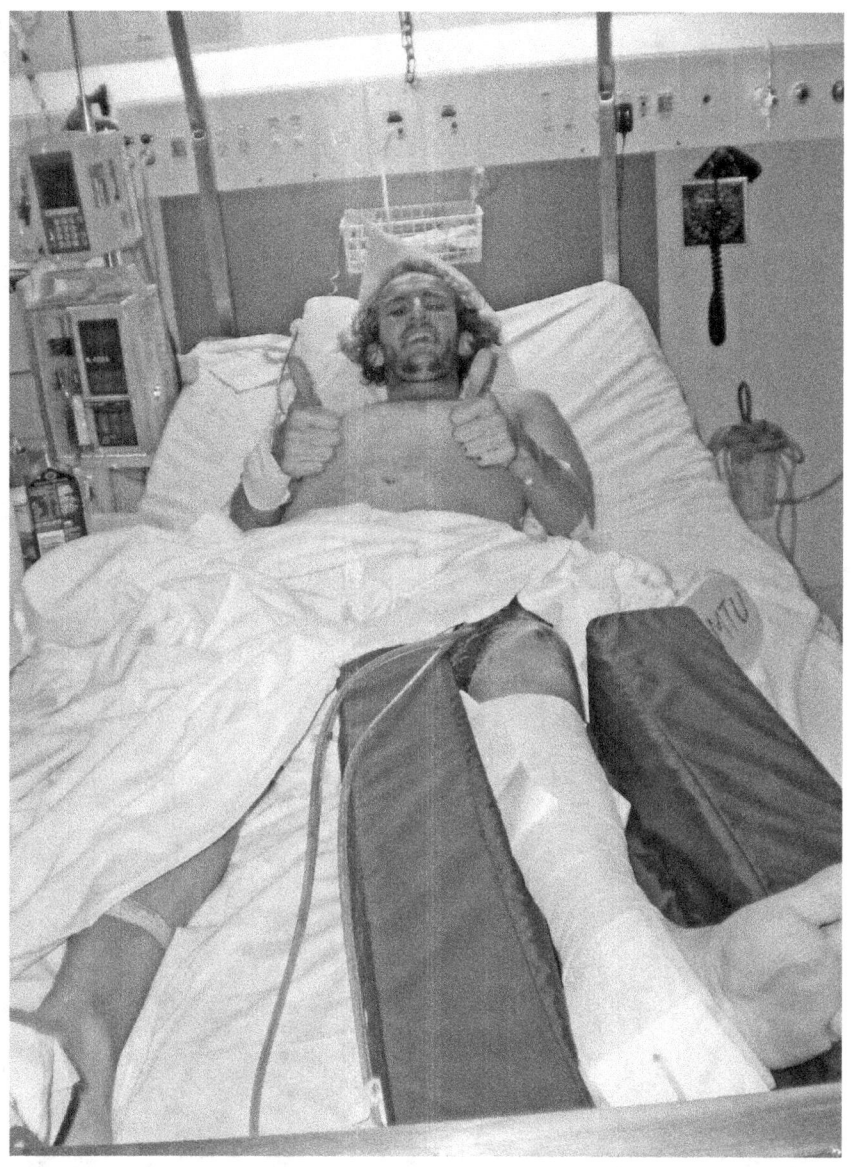

*Everything is fine apparently, because I'm as high as a kite, 20 October 2008!*

*Photo Credit – Allison Slack*

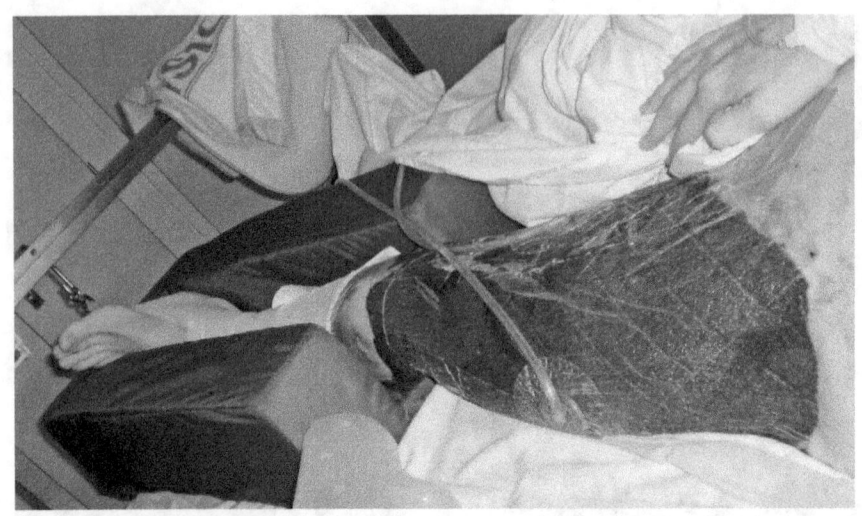

*The Vacuum Dressing; the splint; traction and a pee bottle – These are 4 of my NON-favourite things!*

*Photo Credit – Allison Slack*

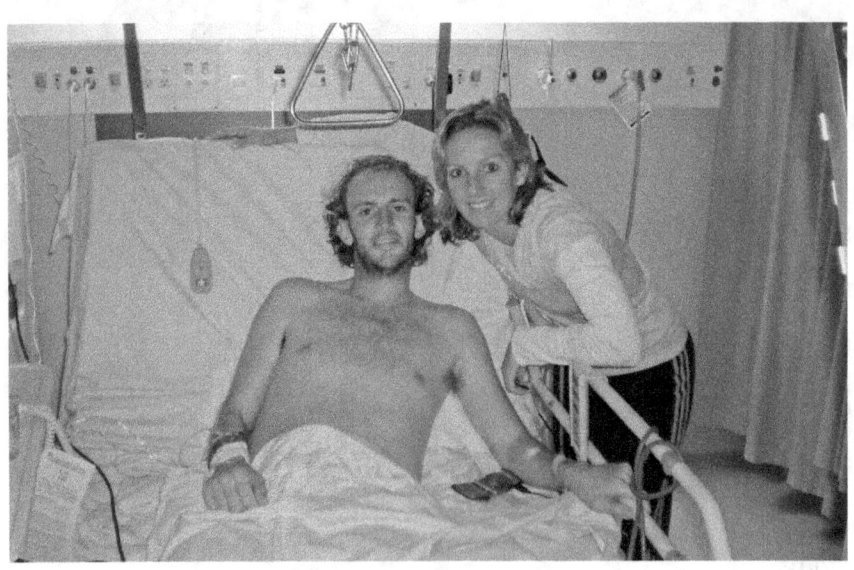

*One of the many visits from Tineke Hancey on 21 October 2008. I've snuck up to more than 30 degrees, for this photo but get busted by the nurse, shortly after Tineke leaves!*

*Photo Credit – Allison Slack*

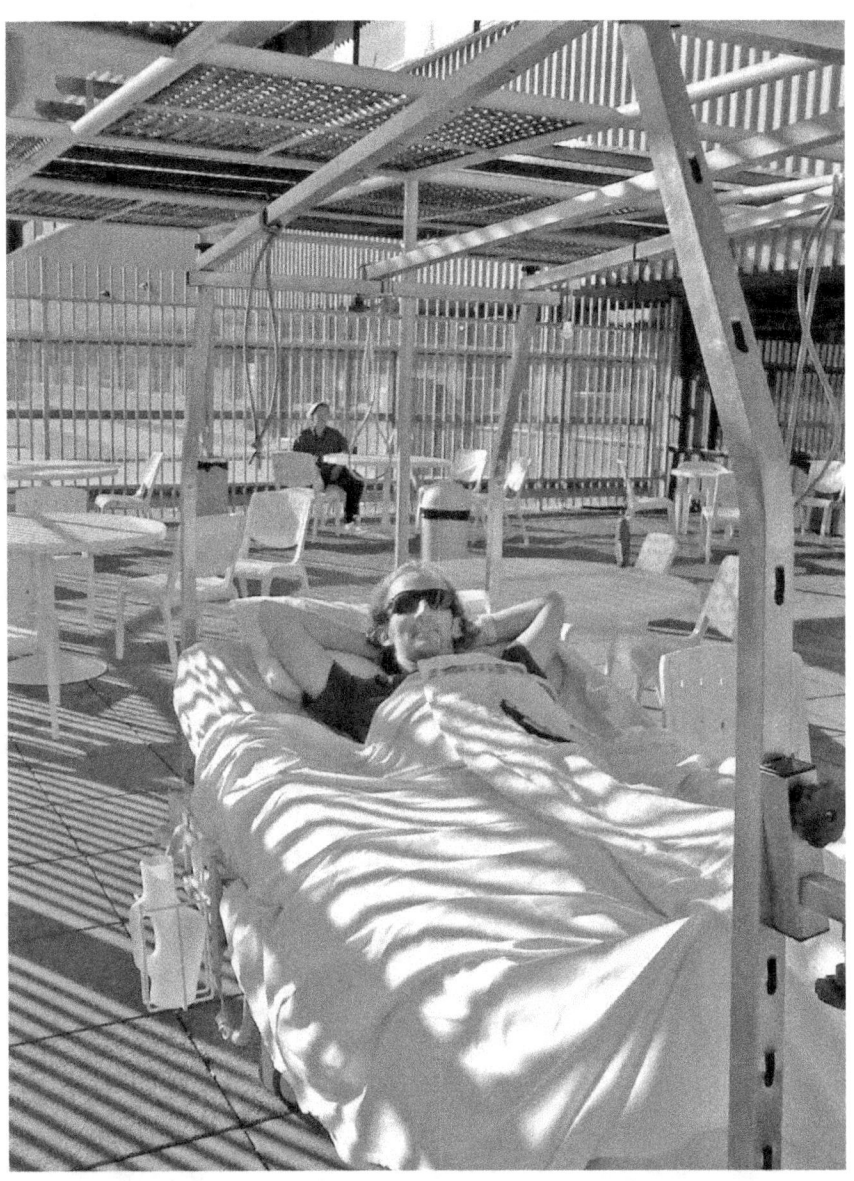

*About a month into my stay at RPH. The balcony on the roof getting some fresh air and a change of scene, on 12 November 2008.*
*Photo Credit – Aidan Midgley*

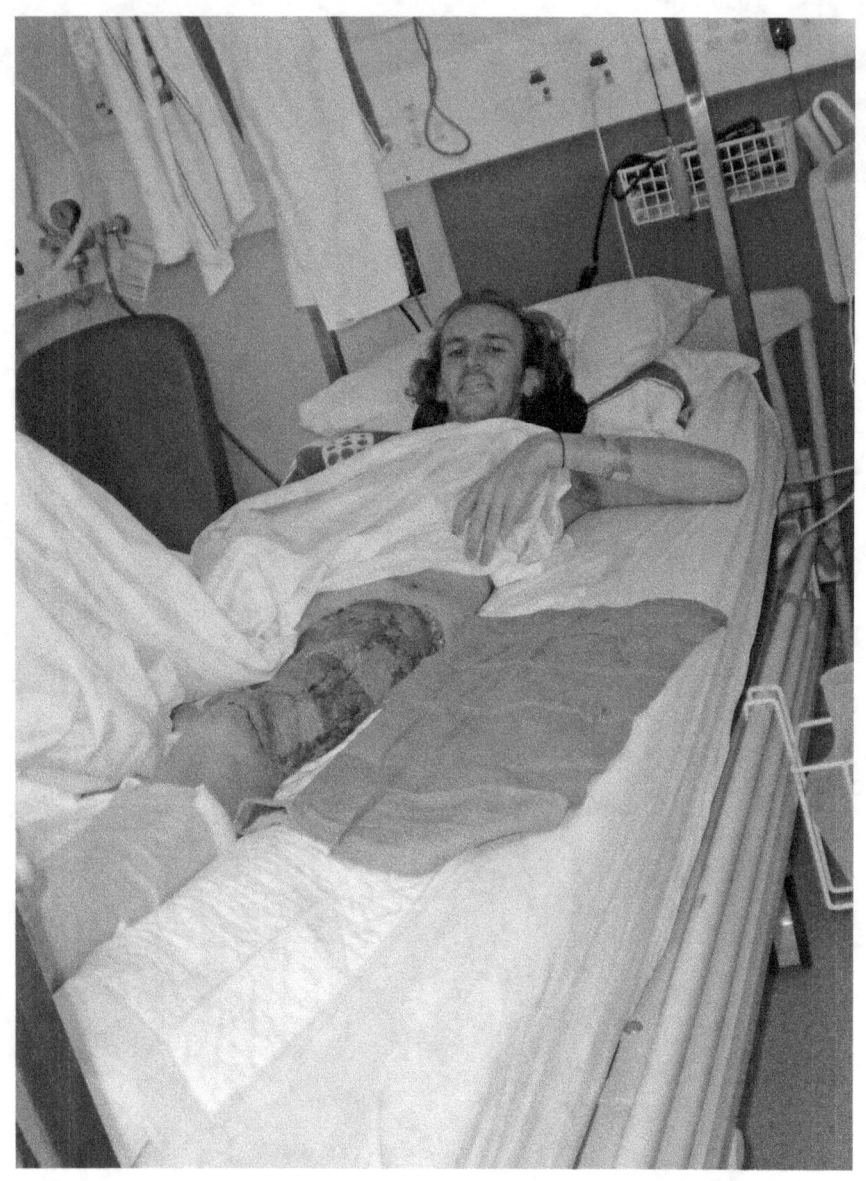

*One of the first dressing changes of my leg that I saw, on 14 November 2008. Not a pretty sight, but other photos are much worse!*
*Photo Credit – Peta McAuliffe*

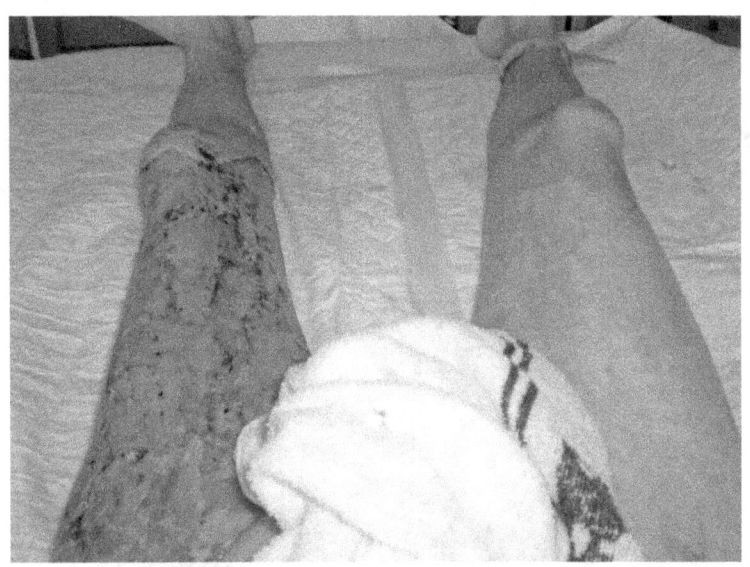

*17 November 2008. My donor-site right leg and my skin-grafted left leg. Cut and paste takes on a whole new meaning!*

*Photo Credit – Peta McAuliffe*

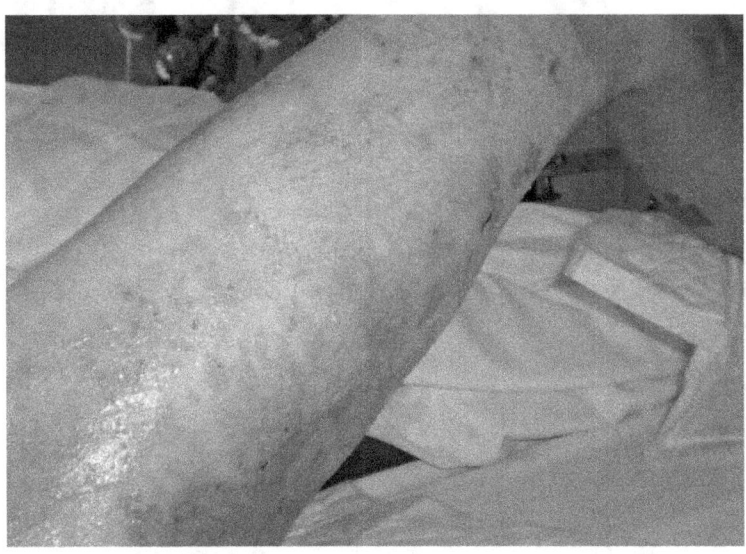

*I was paranoid they were going to take the skin from my entire right leg and I would lose the Ironman tattoo, so it was a relief to see it remained unscathed!*

*Photo Credit – Peta McAuliffe*

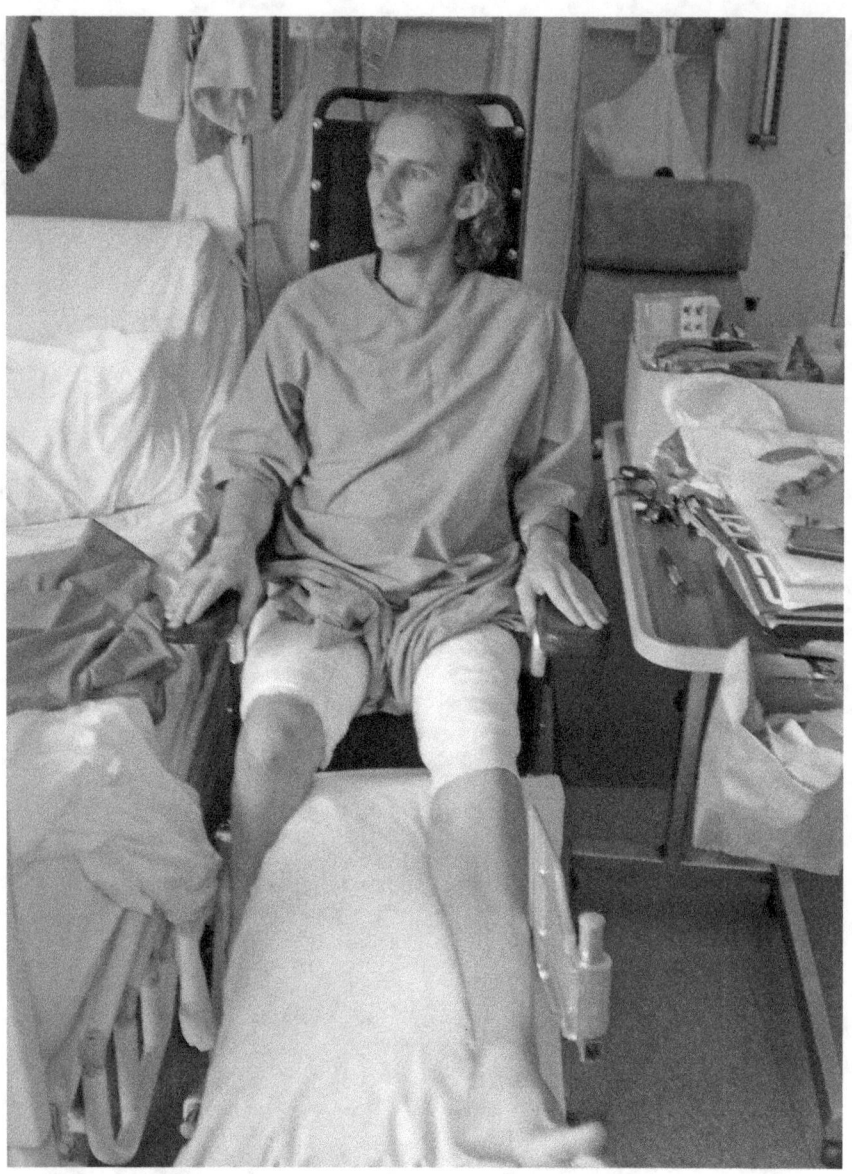

*04 December 2008 at Shenton Park Rehabilitation Campus. The first time in the wheelchair.*

*Photo Credit – Allison Slack*

*In Busselton for IMWA, relaxing on the Higgins's front lawn, watching the cyclists go past. Allison Slack is on the left with Ben, Julie and Louis Bray on the right.*

*Photo Credit – Belinda Higgins*

*Not everyone in Busselton was pleased to see me! Mia Liedermoy had had enough and was telling me all about it!*

*Photo Credit – Belinda Higgins*

*Steve Anstee giving us a wave during his marathon run for his team 'In It To Win It'.*

*Photo Credit – Belinda Higgins*

*Busselton Cycle Club 2008 The "Gravel Rash" Award. My favourite award ever, thanks to my friends' sick sense of humour. Ironically ASADA also stands for Australian Sports Anti-Doping Authority. Credit goes to Neville Sunderland and Andy Milne for this master piece.*

*Photo Credit – Steve Crenfeldt*

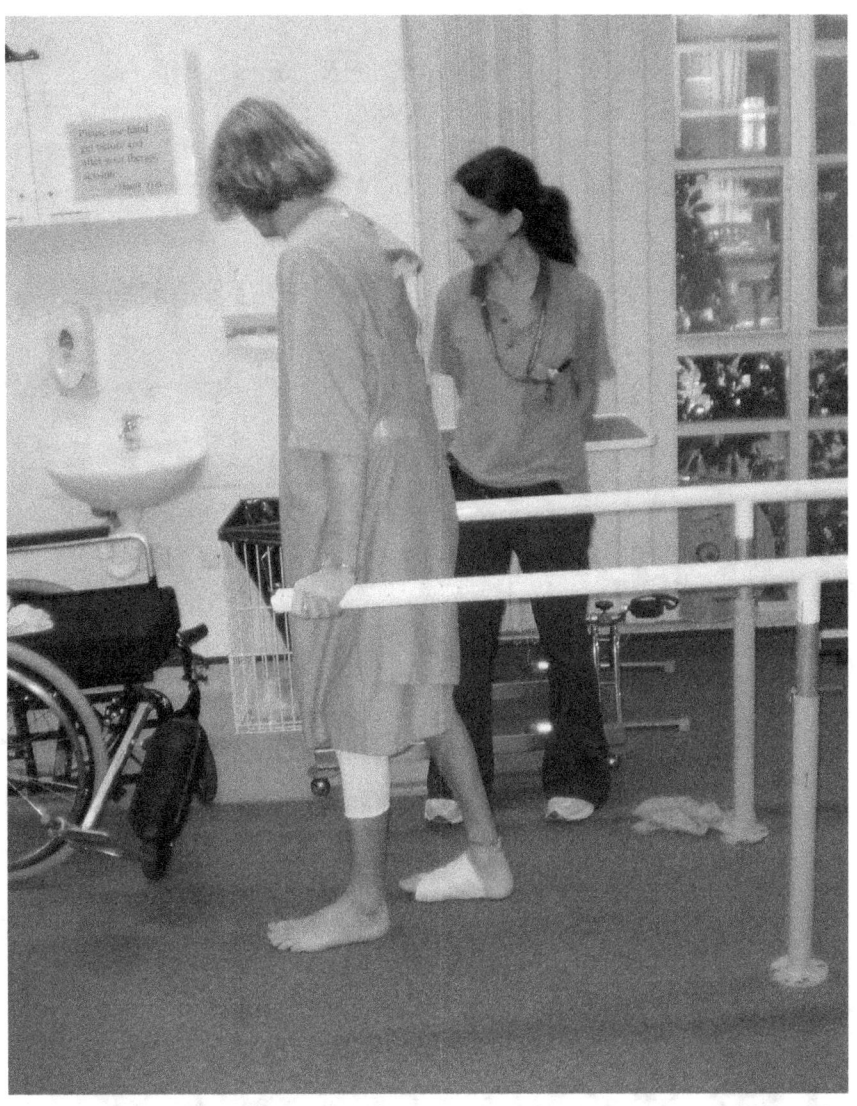

*18 December 2008. Walking exercises, in the Physio Gym of Shenton Park Rehabilitation Campus. Teaching the muscles how to do things again.*

*Photo Credit – Louis Bray*

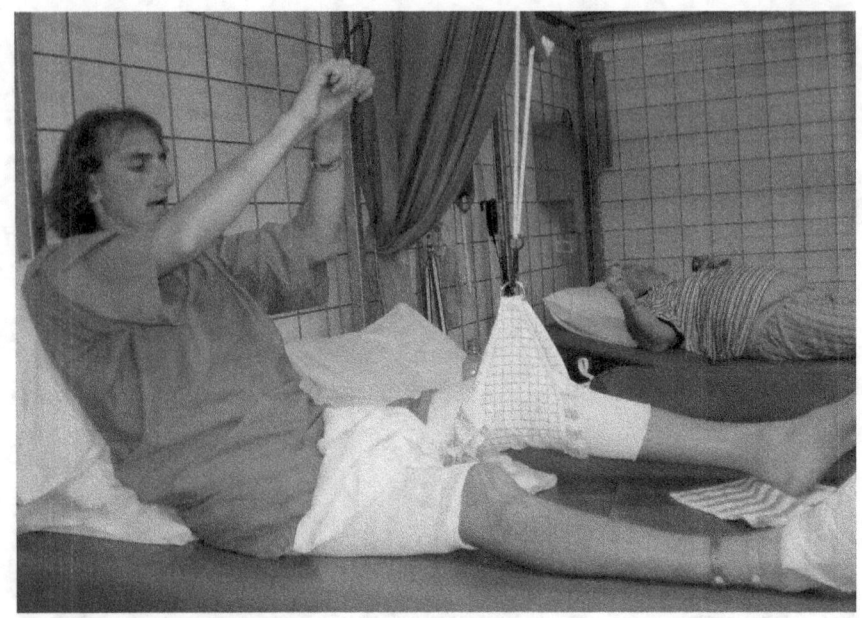

*Leg exercises after my walk, with the full amount of bend I had - approximately 20 degrees.*

*Photo Credit – Louis Bray*

*Dinner with the Bray boys on 19 December 2008. Louis has already half-finished his meal and we haven't even started ours! Nothing much has changed!*

*Photo Credit – Steve Crenfeldt*

*Christmas Day 2008 with Allison's family, relaxing with her cousin Mike Taylor. Wearing the shirt that summed up my situation and how I felt to a tee!*

*Photo Credit – Allison Slack*

*Thank You Drinks on 09 February 2009 and I had the crowd's undivided attention. No one's crying – yet!*

*Photo Credit – Allison Slack*

*Saying a few words…in between a few tears. Wearing my Second Skins compression pants.*

*Photo Credit – Allison Slack*

*Another favourite photo. Peta McAuliffe; Allison Slack and Rosemary Purdie - my "wife and two sisters".*

*Photo Credit – Steve Crenfeldt*

*Aidan Midgley and I sharing a long overdue beer!*

*Photo Credit – Allison Slack*

# 13

# The Land Of The Long White Cloud

*Make no little plans; they have no magic to stir anyone's blood.*
*Make big plans, aim high in hope and work.*
**Daniel H. Burnham**

On Sunday 10 May, I left for New Zealand and was soon back home, spending time with my family and friends, most of whom I hadn't seen since March 2008, when I was back for IMNZ.

Probably the best trait that I have inherited from my parents is doing things for others and helping people, which they always seemed to be doing, as far back as I can remember. I don't think I could ever match the effort that Mum and Dad have put in throughout their lives, but I am pleased to have this as one of my better qualities. Both Mum and Dad are still very active in their church back home in Taupo and Dad has been a member of the Kiwanis Service Club, helping on the committee a number of times over the years. Dad even volunteers for the Ironman in Taupo every year too. When my Nana was alive, back in the late 90's Mum would visit her most evenings in the retirement home where she lived. When she passed away, Mum was offered a job there, as she had spent so much time with Nana, she practically worked there anyway.

My eldest sister, Michelle and her husband, Tim, had planned on having a rugby team of boys, when their first child Jackson was born. The sport quickly changed to netball, after Hayley arrived, who was followed by twins Emily and Katie. Four children obviously weren't enough, so they opened their home to another little girl, who needed a stable and caring environment to grow up in. Samantha has given them just about every positive and negative experience you could imagine, in her short life so far, and seeing how she has changed over the years into a lovely little girl through the love and encouragement from their family reminds me how patient and compassionate Michelle and Tim are. Aimee arrived before the legalities of Samantha's adoption were finalised, so needless to say that with six kids running around, they are very, very busy! Around August 2010, a tumour was discovered on the back of Aimee's head, which resulted in chemotherapy and weeks in hospital in Auckland. Thankfully, the doctors were able to remove everything and she has made a full recovery, which we are all very grateful for.

Our middle sister, Allison and her husband, Bevan married young and have outlasted all of the critics who said they would never stay together. With their 20 year wedding anniversary in 2011, they are still going strong and now have three fantastic children to complete the family. Jordan is all grown up and will soon be off exploring the world, while James and Peyton still have several years of school to get through and plenty more time to remind their parents that three kids are plenty. Allison really took charge during my time in hospital and was constantly after updates and progress reports of my condition. I don't know how she managed to restrain herself and not drive straight to the airport when she first got the news.

Landing in Auckland it was a few nights at Dean and Juls Spittle's house, old friends from Wairakei Resort days, before my sister, Allison, arrived from Hamilton to pick me up. We then drove to her place to spend some time with her family. Another emotional reunion as we just relaxed and enjoyed the company, without having to do too much. Then it was on to Taupo to see Mum and Dad again and my eldest sister Michelle and her family.

On the drive down to Taupo, I found a bike frame to replace the Time Trial bike that was destroyed in the crash. I could barely even rotate my leg on a stationary bike yet, and here I was looking at a new machine! But the signs to buy it were everywhere and reaffirmed my belief in the Law of Attraction, that if you put ideas out there, often they come to fruition! This frame would spend the next several months in the bike room, back in Busselton and then at Fitzroy Cycles in Bunbury, as it was built up ready for me. I just had to get to a point that I could ride it.

While in Taupo, most of my time was divided between Mum and Dad's place and Michelle and Tim's house. With their children being a bit younger, they had the innocence of youth and were not afraid to show plenty of physical affection and were climbing all over me, any chance they got. As far as they were concerned, I had a sore leg, but it was a bit hard for them to grasp the seriousness of it all and didn't understand why they couldn't jump all over me like they did the last time I was home. Luckily the energetic ones were only small, so I wasn't left with any extra damage from all the attention. Again, it was great being able to relax with my family and enjoy the short time we had together, before I had to go home. And like my parents when they visited me, it was beneficial to be able to explain to my sister's families the details of what happened and for them to hear from me first hand as opposed to all of the second hand information they had been getting during the first few months.

The family reunions were very emotional, understandably and were both physically and mentally exhausting, as well as therapeutic at the same time. While I was repeating the same story over and over again to different members of the family and close friends, it was reassuring to know that they could finally understand and relate more to what they thought they knew from the information they were getting at the time. Until they saw me and my injuries, not many people really 'got it'. Often, their idea of what happened and how injured I was, was nowhere near what actually took place. Also by only getting information second hand, which was changing daily, it's not surprising. Again, the not knowing aspect for my family must have been absolutely terrible. Having to meet my friends through phone conversations, discussing a family member who just about died would be indescribable. I can't even imagine what things would have been like for them at the time.

During my time in New Zealand, I had big plans to do some 'secret training' and get back on the bike myself. The few attempts

I had were successful, but it was so sore and uncomfortable that I knew it was still too early. As you can probably appreciate, spending time socializing with my friends became more of a priority!

Another reason why I chose this time to go to New Zealand was also to attend a wedding that I had planned to go home for, before the accident. Janey Duncan and her fiancé Chris Chamberlain were finally tying the knot after several years together. This was a terrific opportunity to catch up with them both, plus I got to see Janey's family again as well. Two of her best friends Debbie Lepper and Nicole Quinton had become very good friends of mine as well, over the years, so it was an added bonus seeing them all together. Great food, fine wine and an awesome occasion with fabulous company made it another weekend of highlights and memories to take back to Australia with me.

I don't get across to New Zealand as frequently as I used to, but still have daily thoughts of my family and it is great being able to Skype each other as often as we like. Mum and Dad have done very well in raising us kids, even though we have all given them plenty of grief over the years. I reckon I am in the lead so far!

Some people questioned why none of my family made the trip across to see me in hospital. As I have said earlier I would have loved having my family around me, when things were at their worst, however, being there with me wouldn't have changed or improved anything. I knew that everybody was worried about me and I knew they cared about me, so that was all that mattered. Logically and financially it just would not have been worth it, especially when I was in a stable condition from quite early on and there was nothing they could have done. Dad and Allison were prepared to jump on a plane straight away, regardless of the reassurances from the doctors and my friends that they didn't need to. I was not upset or disappointed they didn't, because I was often the main person telling them not to come. I know this was the right decision and I am confident that none of my family feels like they should have done more or came across despite my opinion. All of my family did a fantastic job of supporting and caring for me from New Zealand

## The Land Of The Long White Cloud

and were confident that the people I had around me, were doing everything they could.

*A loving atmosphere in your home is
the foundation for all success.*
**Kim DeHaven**

# 14

# Back In The Saddle

*Progress always involves risk; you can't steal second base with your foot still on first.*
**Frederick B Wilcox**

My first proper ride of a bicycle occurred on Thursday 04 June 2009. I had arrived back from New Zealand the day before and had organised to meet Andy Milne at The Goose Café car park at 6:00 a.m. When deciding to go for my first ride, there was really only one guy who it was going to be with. Andy's experience has seen him avoid many crashes and incidents, over his many years of cycling and knowing he was nearby gave me an added confidence that is almost hard to describe. It was as if having him there meant that nothing could go wrong. I knew Andy would ride at my pace, keep me protected from the wind, but still get me out of my comfort zone enough to install some confidence back in me that I could do this. He was my wingman, but he was also there to push me mentally, when I would begin to have my own doubts.

I was given the nickname of Shaggy by Andy, back in 2006, shortly after I started working at Kym Nisbet's Carpet Choice. I had longer hair back then, which was a bit scruffy, so add to that selling Shag-Pile carpet (a popular style that most people think of) and you have a name that I hear more often than Steve on most days. There are many people in Busselton who didn't actually know what my real name was for quite a while. This isn't helped by my friends, who often introduce me as Shaggy on most occasions too. There have been a couple of variations over time including Shags, Shaggy Balls and Shag Dog. However, Scott Munro's Shag Dog Millionaire does have a nice ring to it! And contrary to the belief of

## A Long Ride Back

some who think that it must obviously have some reference to sex, I can assure you that it doesn't and that Shaggy is just an innocent nickname, so stop being rude!

I was using my Giant road bike to ride on, which I had had for several years and was the bike I did my first triathlons of any distance on. I had replaced my shoes and got new cycling knicks to wear. The one thing I had forgotten to replace yet was my bike helmet. When I informed Andy of this, he told me that he had a spare one that I could use. The joke was on me though, when Andy produced a bright pink, feminine helmet for me to wear. So I put it on, did it up and off we went. Just as we were leaving, Max, who was heading out by himself, arrived. Needless to say, he changed his plans and came with us. Andy's plan was to conquer any psychological fears I had. Riding was of course the first one. Riding with others was the second; and riding through the accident scene was the third. With Max and Andy in front, blocking the wind, I was still struggling to keep up with the speed of 25 kmph. We cruised out towards the other cyclists coming back from their ride. We reached the roundabout on Layman road (which had been nicknamed 'Shaggy's roundabout' in my honour), turned around and headed back to town, riding through 'ground zero' shortly after. No major issue to worry about but the skid mark from the truck was clearly visible on the road and is still there today. We then rode back to The Goose Cafe, the ride lasting less than 45 minutes. But it was a success and we all knew that there would be more rides to come.

Two days later, I headed out again, by myself this time, for another short 30 minute ride. The following Tuesday, Andy and I were joined by Joel Nisbet and Dave Fleming and we progressed a little further this time, managing about an hour of riding time. Seeing me back on the bike brought tremendous joy to my fellow cyclists and friends, even though there were still plenty of people around town who were surprised that I had got back on a bike and others who told me that I shouldn't get back on a bike.

One of the goals with getting back to cycling was to ride in a group again, without freaking out. Andy and I would start riding by ourselves, heading out towards the groups coming in from their morning ride. When we saw them coming in the distance, we would turn around and head home, hoping to jump on the back as they rode past.

With one of the first rides that we did this on, the group was flying along, probably sitting on around 40 kmph. Michael and Kym were in the group and recognised that it was Andy and I ahead who had turned around in front of them. They quickly called for the pace to be dropped, knowing that Andy would be setting me up to join them. This drop in pace was just enough for us to get up to their speed and hook on as they over took us.

Andy would take the front and increase the speed. As the group came past, we then joined onto the back and carried on with them. Here, we were getting a good draft, so we could keep up, but still had to work hard. Andy would make sure I was in the right position for this, so I wasn't working any harder than I had to. Once the others riders in the group saw that I was a part of the peloton, the pace was kept nice and steady to help me out as much as possible. I also had the reassurance of knowing that being the last rider, there was nothing coming along behind me.

We did this on a few occasions and on one of these early rides back, the pace was getting quicker and I was riding on pure adrenalin, nothing else. I definitely didn't have the fitness to be doing it, as the pace was well over 30 kmph, probably closer to 35 kmph or slightly higher. The group was starting to split up and those who couldn't keep up were moving to the left. Andy and I were still hanging on and watching the others drop off. One of the ladies we flew past was Connie, who was very pleased to see me out riding, but was certainly not impressed that I was amongst the group who dropped her, especially with my very recent return to riding. We laughed about it afterwards, but at the time, she was not happy!

Slowly the riding distances increased as did the frequency I was getting out there, even though the cold winter mornings kept Andy and me consistently inconsistent. One Saturday afternoon ride on

## A Long Ride Back

15 August 2009, Andy decided it was time to ride the Alps. By this of course, he meant heading up Sues Hill, a climb of around 3 km, which has a 3% gradient. I was very hesitant about doing this, as I didn't feel fit enough to try such a task yet, but Andy wasn't having any of it. Much to my surprise and relief, I made it up without too much trouble, but again, I think it was more adrenalin that actual ability.

These rides continued over the next few weeks, as I slowly increased both the distance and my fitness slowly began to improve, but not to any great length yet. I knew this was going to be a slow process, but the frustrations of being able to ride again, but still not able to keep up with my friends, grew each time. There were many occasions that I considered giving up, because I felt the path to get me back to riding with the group was so long and exhausting, that it was all too hard. I had strategically placed the two photo collages I had in hospital, on the doors of my wardrobe, in the bike room, where I would have to look at them every time I opened it up to get my cycling gear out. This was another reminder to stay motivated for the people who had shown me support and who would be pleased to see me make a successful return to triathlon.

At the same time I was returning to cycling, I was back to increasing my work shifts from a few hours, up to half days and eventually full time by the end of June. My days would usually begin with an hour of physiotherapy before work, which would leave me exhausted by lunchtime initially, but gradually became easier as I got fitter, stronger and more active. Kym and Sharon were very patient and understanding of my rehabilitation and gave me all the time I needed to get back to normal at my own pace.

One thing I became very worried about as I began to improve and became more independent, was having people see me getting around without much difficulty and thinking everything looked okay, without understanding that there was still a lot going on. It would be easy for people to look at me and think that there was nothing wrong with me, as I could walk fairly normally by now and was driving again too. I still wasn't working full time though

## Back In The Saddle

and began worrying that some people might think I was faking things, seeing as though I was claiming work subsidised payments, through my Mortgage Protection Insurance. Anyone I spoke to about this, told me not to worry as there was enough to support the fact that I was not back to full normality yet. It was a relief when I was able to go back to full time employment and was working for every dollar I earned.

The riding was short lived as about a month later I had to return to Royal Perth Hospital. But I was pleased with the success I had and the progress I had made. At least I could do it – physically and mentally!

*Success is to be measured not so much by the position one has reached in life as by the obstacles he has overcome while endeavouring to succeed.*
**Booker T. Washington**

# 15

# Solitary Confinement

*Do what you can, where you are, with what you have.*
*Theodore Roosevelt*

I was admitted back into Royal Perth Hospital on Monday 14 September 2009 and had surgery that morning. This was a full thickness skin graft operation on an area behind my knee, which was refusing to heal properly. They sliced between my stomach and my right leg, down towards the groin, took a big piece of meat out and stitched me up again. This piece of flesh was then placed on the area behind my knee, to strengthen it and give a stronger blood supply to assist in the healing. A week later, a second operation was done to finish off the graft. Everything went well and the recovery began. It was a return to the same, as I had to stay in bed, keep my leg straight and not move around too much. Easily done, but very, very boring! At least this time, I was only in a brace and wasn't on traction. This meant I even got to have a shower or two and could also use the bathroom! The downside of being a regional patient in the city was that I had to stay in hospital in case I needed urgent care. If I had lived in Perth however, I would have been able to go home and come back every few days or sooner if required. I was fortunate to be allowed out for the weekend, over 26 and 27 September and was lucky enough to stay at Kate, Dylan and Jo Wilson's house. Dylan was only 3 ½ years old at the time and found it very frustrating that I was there to visit, but couldn't play, muck around or wrestle! I had a smaller vacuum dressing on this time, with a portable machine attached to my leg, which I could carry with me, when I walked around. This meant nothing to young Dylan, except for the occasional farting noise it made, which had him laughing regularly of course.

## A Long Ride Back

The vacuum dressing was similar to what I had on my entire upper leg after the accident, but on a much smaller, and painless scale. This was nowhere near as sore as last time and was much more tolerable, requiring only minimal pain relief. After my weekend release from RPH, I was back in on Monday for the surgeons to look at the wound. They were pleased with the progress, but weren't letting me go home just yet.

During this time in RPH, I had a visit from Marcel, the psychologist assigned to me back in 2008. He had seen my name on the medical records and saw that I was back in. He dropped by to say hello and ask how I was going and why I was back in hospital. It was nice that he took the time to do this and we had a good chat about my progress and how I was handling everything. He didn't have to stop by and I am grateful that he took the time out of his day to do so. It was a very nice gesture.

The food in hospital was alright, most of the time, but after a couple of weeks, I had sampled nearly everything on the same rotating menu as last time – yet again and wasn't really on any major drugs to hide the taste of the food. With this, my second stay at RPH, I was getting to the stage where I had had enough. The guy opposite me, Ben McCoy was talking to his girlfriend on the phone one night as she was coming up to visit in a few hours' time. My ears pricked up when he mentioned her bringing in a pizza for him and when she offered to bring some for all of us, we were mad keen! The taste of real food was such a relief after the 2 weeks of mass produced hospital cuisine.

It's funny how we quickly identify the people who we will get on with and can associate freely with. Ben was about 10 years younger than me I think, but we had a couple of elderly patients in the room with us. They were often confused about where they were and why they were in hospital. Unfortunately, there were some nurses who would get frustrated at having to repeat the explanation again and again to these patients and were quite short, sometimes even rude to them. We often found ourselves becoming quite protective of these elderly chaps and would keep an eye on them as best we could.

# Solitary Confinement

Ben eventually got discharged and I was left to hang out with the remaining patients by myself. Late on the Saturday evening, I had a new roommate. I was awoken by him getting settled in and the nurses doing their observations and it was clear that I was going to be awake for a while. I was getting annoyed at being woken up by all the noise and frustrated that I had been having a good sleep. Suddenly, he pulled back the curtain separating us and said 'sorry about the noise man, want some pizza?' He had ordered it not long after he arrived and so we sat in our beds, munching away while watching movies on the TV he had connected up. The second bonus came the next morning when he left early and had paid for 24 hours of TV viewing. His bed didn't get occupied all day, so I was able to watch his TV from my bed! Score!

A few days later, the nurses began doing routine tests on all the patients for bugs and germs such as Staphylococcus Aureus and other nasty things. I was the lucky winner of the testing apparently, as a few hours later I was being moved to my own private room.

It was nothing to do with my snoring or the privilege of being the Ward's best patient for the second visit in a row, I was in isolation because I had MRSA. Methicillin Resistant Staphylococcus Aureus is a bacterial infection that is highly resistant to some antibiotics. MRSA normally lives on the skin and sometimes in the nasal passages of healthy people. It poses no threat to the person who has it or to most people around them. But for people with weak immune systems and the seriously ill patients in hospitals it can be very dangerous.

So as a precaution, I was isolated and every hospital staff member that came into my room, regardless of their role, had to have a gown, gloves and a mask on, which was thrown away when they left. Ironically, I was allowed to leave the room without having to wear these items and my visitors could come in to see me and not have to wear them either. This was one of the many funny rules of the health system that doesn't really make sense. The bonuses to having my own room were that I didn't have to put up with other patient's snoring; noisy machines; or lights being turned on at all hours of the night. It was however, very boring and lonely. Finally, the doctors decided that my skin graft was stable enough for me to go home. Saturday 10 October 2009 concluded my second stay in hospital. I was meant to be in for about a week, but this dragged out to nearly a month.

Having the break from riding for further operations, was actually a good thing. It gave me time to reflect on the success I had had, and gave me a bit more enthusiasm to get back out there again, once I got out of hospital.

Within days of being out, I was back on the bike again, slowly increasing the distances, and building my strength so that soon I would be able to leave with the group and not have to meet them on their way home. My main fear was not being able to keep up and other riders having to go around and avoid me, possibly causing an accident. I was pleased to be back on a bike, but I was also angry that I couldn't do it as well as I could, less than a year ago. I wanted to be faster and stronger instantly.

Within the first 5 km of our weekday loop, there is a short incline up the Cemetery hill, along Vasse Highway. Nothing bad to look at, but when you aren't feeling very fit, it can play games with your mind. It seemed like several weeks went past when I wasn't strong enough to keep up with everybody else and was fading towards the back of the group. Unbeknown to me a lot of those times, Andy would get himself into a position behind me, ready to give me a gentle hand on the back to push me up the slope so I wouldn't get dropped by the group. Andy's riding experience was again invaluable at times like these, blocking the wind or getting me into a position where I could benefit most from the riders around me. Other times it was simply to tell me to push harder and keep up with the rider in front of me. As my confidence began to grow, I knew where I needed to be to get the best draft, but I often didn't have the strength to stay in the right position for very long. The group rides continued and gradually the distances increased, as I aimed to reach 50 km in one ride again.

Solitary Confinement

Just before Christmas 2009, my new Jamis Xenith Time Trial bike was all finished and ready, so I began riding that as much as I could, to get used to being in the aero position again and being on a different bike seat for longer than 30-40 km. This was the frame I had purchased in New Zealand, back in May and had been at the bike shop since. Fitzroy's Cycles had quoted on a replacement bike for my insurance through Cycle Cover, and the cheque was made out to them, so that was where my insurance money would be spent. John Starr, owner of Fitzroy Cycles did a great job of building me a new racing machine with the specific components I wanted on it.

I cannot recommend bike insurance enough to all cyclists and am pleased that many of my friends have since insured their own bikes, after my accident. Having the money to replace the damaged bike certainly helped get me back into cycling and aiming for future goals.

*We are continually faced by great opportunities, brilliantly disguised as insoluble problems.*

**Lee Iacocca**

# 16

# The Magic Of Thinking Big

*Imagination is everything. It is the preview of
life's coming attractions.*
**Albert Einstein**

I'm not sure of the exact time in 2009 that I first thought about entering the 2010 Busselton Half Ironman. These thoughts took place well before I was physically able to consider this challenge as I was not allowed in the water to swim and still only had left knee bend of around 100 degrees. I couldn't run and wasn't even on the bike then. But as the year went on, I began thinking more about it and wondered if it would be possible. The conclusion was that it would all depend on the swim. If I was allowed in the water by the end of January 2010 at the latest, I would give it a go. If not, then not to worry, I would refocus on 2011. I knew that I would be able to reach the 1.9 km distance if I could begin swimming by that time and 90 km of riding was easily achievable. But getting close to running 21 km, in four months? That would be the tester. To make things worse, entries would fill up fast when they opened, so if I didn't enter, I would definitely miss out. And what was the point of training if I couldn't do the event?

A lot of people assumed my goal would be the 2010 Ironman. This was easy to say a strong no to as it wasn't even on my radar yet, and when it did appear, the thought was very brief. But the Half Ironman managed to sneak under a lot of other people's radars and the general assumption was that I would do it in a team. I have strong feelings about completing events solo and then going back to being part of a team. For me, it is all or nothing. So if I ever do

## A Long Ride Back

an event like this in a team, it will have to be for some very important reasons or with some very special people.

After a review in December, by Anthony Williams, my Plastic Surgeon, and him telling me that it was my choice as to when I went into the water, I decided upon the second week of January 2010, to begin swimming. The skin graft behind my knee had just about healed, but was still very vulnerable. I wanted to give it a few more weeks, before I began training. Once entries opened, I re-joined Triathlon Western Australia and entered the HIM at the same time. I wrote myself an 18 week program, loosely based on previous years and would fine tune it each month, depending on how I felt. The next step was to email my Coach, Ross and tell him, also asking for his advice. Naturally, he was full of praise for setting the goal and suggested a website by Jeff Galloway who wrote training programs for people getting into running. It was based on walking and running to keep the body fresh and moving at a higher speed, without exhausting the athlete.

Training began with a build-up week on Monday 28 December 2009. I had been going to the gym and physiotherapy, three times per week, so the body was slowly getting used to physical activity again. The running and walking began on this day as well, with one lap of a recreational field, running for 10 seconds and walking for 30 seconds over a period of around 10 minutes. This continued every second day and I slowly built up to running for 30 seconds, walking for 1 minute. Then running for a minute and walking for 2 minutes, slowly increasing time and distance as my body grew stronger.

My first swim was Sunday 10 January 2010. I don't enjoy swimming and seem to put a lot of effort in, for not much of a result, but on this occasion, I just got in and swam. The end result was a very surprising 1 km, in around 1 hour, but I was exhausted for the rest of the day. Even though I hadn't swum for around 15 months, it all came back to me straight away and I could hear Michael's coaching voice in my head, telling me the fundamentals of swimming – reach, pull, keep your head still, kick and the other instructions.

## The Magic Of Thinking Big

As I was back at the gym and was swimming, riding and running as well, even though it was in very small quantities, it was time to stop physiotherapy after more than a year of treatment. Jeff and Katie had been absolutely amazing with my rehabilitation and the support I received from this magical couple could never be equalled or repaid. Even though most of the sessions contained a very high pain level, there was plenty of boisterous laughter coming from the treatment room as Jeff and I entertained each other with stories of years gone by, recent training sessions and the hilarious antics of his two young daughters, Hannah and Lucy. The greatest advantage of having a physiotherapist as well as my GP who cycle themselves, is that if needed, I had a get-out-of-jail-free card to use, if the body decided that the HIM wasn't going to happen. I had no intentions of using this, but it was reassuring to know that if my body didn't allow training to continue, I had people who knew that I had put the effort in to try.

So training continued as I slowly built up the distances for each discipline. By the end of January, I was swimming 1.5 km, riding 55 km and running and walking 5 km. It wasn't fast and it wasn't pretty, but it was a start. Cycling was the easier of the three, but as the speed increased, the lungs were burning during each ride, as I tried to stay with the group I was in, until eventually I would get spat out the back and watch them disappear into the distance, as I rode home alone, unless I was lucky enough to be picked up by other riders coming past.

I tried not to advertise the fact that I had entered the HIM. If people asked, I would tell them yes, but it wasn't going to be posted on Facebook – yet! The first week in February is the Busselton Jetty Swim and while I was nowhere near ready for the 3.6 km round trip, the shorter 1 km option became the first major goal of 2010. I hadn't done any ocean swimming until the day, so it would be interesting to see how I would go.

I was training in full length swimming trunks, from the waist down. With a massively skin grafted thigh, I wasn't keen on showing this off to the world yet, maybe not ever. Changing in public was always a stealth operation to avoid the looks and stares and questions, even from my friends, who I knew didn't care what it looked like, but I was self-conscious of anyway. I wore the same suit for the 1 km swim, with a few people who didn't know what I was trying to hide, giving me grief for wearing a 'speed-suit'. It didn't bother me and besides, I needed all the help I could get. I knocked the distance off in just less than 30 minutes, which for where I was in my training, was pleasing enough for me.

Joined by my good friend Brad Goldsmith, as well as Simon Mansfield and Pat Bromell from the Busselton Jetty Swim Committee, the four of us all finished at nearly exactly the same time and were never far from each other throughout the swim, even if we didn't all realise it at the time. Brad has done the Jetty swim countless times and makes the 3.6 km distance look easy, but had told me that whatever swim I was doing, he was doing. We had been part of a team for the 2008 swim and as far as he was concerned, he wasn't doing anything until I was swimming with him. Again, one of the kind and humbling gestures that many of my friends made to welcome me back into my sport.

So the swim was over and the latest goal was achieved. Riding resumed a few days later and after biting off more than I could chew, an extended ride with Connie and Wendy saw me hit the wall big time and struggle back to town to finish an 85 km ride. This turned out to be the longest ride I had done since October 2008. I was feeling absolutely stuffed and after my customary hot chocolate, it was home to spend the afternoon sleeping! A few hours later I woke up in a world of pain and could hardly stand. Sensing that something wasn't quite right, I called Aidan and asked him to take me to hospital. It turned out that I had an infection behind my knee, on one of the small areas which hadn't quite healed properly. We don't know exactly what caused it, but the ocean was our main suspect, during the Busselton Jetty Swim. After a few more days in Busselton Hospital on some serious antibiotics, I was allowed out to recover and take it easy. Tony Best, my GP, recommended not swimming for another week, however. Now the demons in my head started telling me that I didn't have enough time to reach the distance required for May's HIM. If I expended too much energy in the swim, I would suffer on the ride and not have enough time to complete the 21 km run. I had only reached about 6 km so far, and was aiming to run at least 10 km, hopefully more. All I could do was keep training and see what happened. As long as I didn't get sick again, I should be fine. If necessary, I wouldn't swim until the day, but that wasn't a scenario I was happy with.

The answer lay in the bike, so it was back to the program to keep myself steadily and consistently riding distances of between 80 km–100 km. Riding the ton on a regular basis had built my strength and endurance over the years, so I knew that I had to start there to build it up again. Not being able to keep up with other cyclists over a distance of around 100 km meant that most of these had to be done by myself. There were a few contenders on some occasions and Andy was dragged along far too often than he would have liked. I kept persisting with the running and used the gym to try to add some muscle somewhere, anywhere.

At the end of January 2010, I had decided to leave Carpet Choice, in the hopes of finding work with a local paper, as a journalist. The majority of my friends told me that I was good at writing; particularly sports articles and that I should pursue this as a career option. Possible leads turned out to be dead ends and a month passed where I was out of work completely. Money was running out and it didn't look like there was anything on the horizon. I was getting pretty desperate and dropped off my CV to a lot of businesses around Busselton in the hopes of picking up any work I could. There was always talk that local businesses were looking for staff, but any enquiries to the specific places were met with the same answer – sorry, nothing available. I even got rejected by The Reject Shop! How's that for confidence shattering!

I had been at Carpet Choice for about 4 years and couldn't see selling floor coverings as what I wanted to do any more. Kym and Sharon had been incredibly supportive and very accommodating with the amount of time off I had and easing me back into work after I had recovered. But I also knew it wasn't fair to them to keeping working there when my heart wasn't in it and wasn't fair on myself to be doing something I wasn't enjoying anymore. Even though it would mean Kym having to do more until the new staff were up to speed, they understood how I felt. This couple has been terrific to me over the years and are another set of 'parents' I have managed to accrue since living in Busselton.

I soon began thinking I had made a very big mistake. The plan of having more time to train for the HIM and possible part time work to keep the bills paid did not work and while still on antibiotics for a few weeks after the infection, I didn't have the energy to utilise this extra training time to my advantage. It was all looking very grim and I could feel myself heading down hill. Luckily, an opportunity came along to give me nearly exactly what I wanted, except for the million dollar salary of course.

Purds was working at Busselton Fresh IGA Supermarket and suggested I apply for an upcoming vacancy there. After an interview with the owners, I was hired! Here, I could work 5 afternoons a week and have the mornings to train. It involved supervising the shop's operation, keeping the after school kids working and trying to prevent the amount of shoplifting that occurred, as it does in most retail businesses. The hours were convenient, the pay was keeping the wolf from the door again and it gave me a little bit of lifestyle as well. I would start in the early afternoon and finish around 7:30 p.m. – 8:30 p.m. at night. This was still early enough to catch up with friends for dinner, see a movie or general socialising, but most importantly, allow me to get back into my training for the HIM.

During their training, most of my friends were doing the same sort of program and adding in the Western Australia State Tri Series races as well, with some including Ironman Australia in Port Macquarie. Choosing not to swim in the ocean meant I couldn't do these smaller races and the frustration of not being able to participate with them was really starting to get to me. While they planned road trips to Perth, Bunbury and Albany and were getting good results, I was struggling to run or walk for more than an hour.

# The Magic Of Thinking Big

When I started training at the beginning of the year, my goal was to finish before the cut off time of 7 ½ hours. I would have been happy with crossing the line in 7:29:59. The running improved steadily through February and March and I was able to run, without walking for 7 km in about 1 hour. My longest run was for 2 hours solid, a distance of about 14 km. This distance left my body in a lot of pain, from my knees, up to my hips and lower back. I had only achieved half the distance I needed to and was fighting with myself over whether or not it would be enough. The decision was made that that was as long as I would run for until race day. This gave me a potential run time of 3 hours for 21 km. With a 50 minute swim and 3 hour ride, the new time to aim for was 06:59:59. Several weeks of over 100 km rides were helping my base fitness increase, but I didn't think I could ride sub 3 hours on race day. Anyone I shared this thought with however, disagreed.

Then I reread a book called The Magic Of Thinking Big by David J Schwartz. It's an old book but is still relevant today as it takes any situation you are in and helps you to move towards the goals you want to achieve. I have always liked books and movies about the underdog or overcoming adversity, but most of them either have a Hollywood storyline and end with the individual or team winning the title. These would frustrate me, as I was never out to win. I was only out to complete the journey and cross the finish line. But through reading the book again, I set a new goal and grew confident every day that I could reach it. I never wanted to advertise it of course, but 06:29:59 was the new target. That was based on a 40 min. swim / 2:50 hr. ride / 3:00 hr. run including transitions. I only told a handful of people about this goal, two of whom were Jeff and Katie.

*If you have a dream, give it a chance to happen.*
***Rich DeVos***

# 17

# The Starter's Gun

*The man who wins, may have been counted out several times,
but he didn't hear the referee.*

### H. E. Jansen

A highlight of the 2010 HIM was having my best friend Rick Keehan, come over from New Zealand to watch and support me on race day. Having lived and worked in Busselton before, it was also a chance for him to catch up with old friends; have a holiday and check out the local delicacies around the region. It was very cool having him here and the closest thing to my New Zealand family I had. I was always grateful that Rick was the one to deliver the news of my accident to my parents, not someone from Busselton that they didn't know. Rick brought well wishes from home, presents and a few tasty treats as well. We have been mates for over 10 years and had travelled around the world on holiday together in 2003. We had worked together in New Zealand, England and here in Busselton. I have been trying to convince him and his fiancée to move here for years, but haven't been successful yet. With his sporting background as a champion swimmer in his youth, he understood the discipline of my training and preparation for my race. He was also good at keeping me relaxed, helping me not to stress and making sure there was plenty of laughter going on all the time. He also made sure that I was replenishing my carbohydrate levels at the awards party afterwards!

I woke at 3:00 a.m. on Saturday 01 May 2010. I had planned to get up at 5:00 a.m. so was not happy to be awake this early. A quick check of Facebook after breakfast and I began to get ready. By 5:30 a.m. I had my head over the toilet bowl, and had lost everything

## A Long Ride Back

I had eaten. The nerves hit hard and I wasn't feeling too flash. We headed to transition to lay everything out and prepare for the start of the race. I said good luck to a few people I saw and had a quick chat to Ross. He could tell I was freaking out, so told me to relax, breathe, have fun and left me to it.

I walked toward the beach with Rick, Allison, Jo and a few others to wait for my wave start. After hugs and good lucks from a few friends, I headed to the water. A starter's gun went off in the background and I looked across to see a bunch of wetsuits with yellow caps running into the water. Shit! I was wearing a yellow cap! I walked under the little jetty on the right to confirm my suspicions and my heart sank as I was behind already. But for some reason, I wasn't too worried. Sure, I wasn't going to find feet to draft off, but I just walked in, dived under and aimed for the first buoy. I had clear open water in front of me and had avoided the washing machine effect of mass starts. After about 500 metres, I began passing the stragglers of my wave. If I was catching these guys, they must be slow! I swam the rest of the way by myself, until the final 700 metres or so, where the next wave of swimmers caught me. From here, I just jumped on each set of feet as they sped past and drafted back to the beach. I had no idea of my swim time and the clock was displaying when the first wave started, so this didn't help me. Through transition and I was soon getting on the bike. I heard the announcer call Michael's name, so I knew he would be passing me soon.

Out of transition and onto the bike, along Geographe Bay Road. Max and Jenny Higgins' house is about 1 km from the start and is usually a gathering point for local spectators to cheer on the competitors they know. I didn't wash the saltwater out of my mouth enough and was coughing and spluttering as I tried to take my first drink, not far from this point. Suddenly a familiar voice was behind me. 'Welcome back Shaggy Balls, it's good to have you back out here with us.' It was Michael smashing past me and as soon as I heard his voice, I began crying, listening to what he said and how cool it was, that he was the first person I knew to come past me. With all the emotions over flowing, I was still trying to be-

## The Starter's Gun

gin my nutrition program. Big mistake! The gels I ate came straight back up and so did the liquid I was drinking. Less than 2 km into the ride, I was vomiting all over myself and trying to ride at the same time. I gave up the nutrition for now and began reading my race day mantras, which were stuck between my tri-bars. My aim now was a 30 kmph average, but anything I ate or drank was lost straight away. I didn't eat anything until after the turnaround point, about 22.5 km from town.

It was about 25 km into the race that I managed to keep a small piece of banana down, so I thought I might be okay. Protein bar pieces stayed down sometimes and I got a couple of gels in me, but it was nowhere near the amounts that I should have been eating. I saw Ross in the Higgins' driveway and gave him a yell as I headed out on my second and final lap of the bike. I started feeling a little better by this stage and was drinking some fluid and keeping down a little bit more food. At the turnaround point, I could see more of the competing Busselton locals including Max and Connie behind me. My next plan was to finish the bike leg, before Max caught me. My picnic box food was still full by the end of the ride and I hadn't even finished one bottle of fluid. But I continued riding hard and achieved the goals of a 30 kmph average speed and had made it back to transition before Max passed me, so I was happy.

I hit transition and changed shoes. Grabbed my bag of goodies and walked out toward the road. Cap on, gloves off, fuel belt on, race number belt turned around and I began to run as soon as my foot hit the tar seal. Just then Max ran past, congratulating me as well. My support crew was waiting and I ditched the bag of unwanted items on the way through. The goal now was to keep running the entire distance and not walk at all. A quick toilet stop, which I thought might be my downfall, was over with and a time check said 25 min for 3.5 km. Ahead on run time already, but still a long way to go. The only people I passed on the run were walkers. I was feeling okay, but was starving. My body wanted food and all I had was gels and energy drink. But I knew if I just kept going, I would soon be at the finish line and it would be all over. At the half way point, my run time said 1:25 hr. I was well ahead

## A Long Ride Back

of finishing under 7 hours, and 6 ½ hours was looking achievable. One by one, most of the competitors I knew ran past me, all offering me support and congratulations for making it to race day. I was returning the favour for as many as I could, as well as encouraging the walkers, by telling them it was time to run again for a little while.

Ben Bray ran past on his last lap, looking strong on his way to completing his first HIM. Not long after, a familiar voice was shouting at me again – 'Shaggy Balls! - Looking good mate!' It was Michael, but I had a response this time – 'Green Cap, just ahead, I think he's yours'. Michael looked up and recognised his son, Ben. 'You're right, he's mine!' he replied and headed off in pursuit. The final 3.5 km was soon there and I broke it down to the 4 stages once again. First was the Higgins' house; then the aid station; the Watson's house; then the Marine Sea Rescue Building where we hold our Busselton Triathlon Club events. After that was the finish chute with plenty of support marquees in between. Some of the crew from the Bunbury Triathlon Club recognised me and cheered me along as well, which added to the emotion and realisation that I was just about to finish a successful return to HIM triathlon. I was running at a great pace for me and was finishing strong, just like my game plan. The finishing chute began on the grass and I thought I was going to collapse as the surface changed underneath me. Around the corner and the clock said just over 6 ½ hours. I knew I had to take time off from when my wave started, so I must have finished just under that time.

I was barely across the line when they put the finisher's medal around me and the weight of it nearly flattened me. They are a decent size and it seemed to weigh so much more when you include the emotion of the day as well. Suddenly, I was surrounded by Busselton locals – Max and Jenny, Connie, Wendy, Melina, Steve Ashworth and Cate Finlay all celebrating my achievement. The legs began to wobble and the parental instincts took over as several arms reached out to make sure I remained standing. It was done! Over! Finished! The official time reading:

## The Starter's Gun

**HIM 2010** — Total - 06:25:37
00:42:06 Swim / 02:50:28 Bike / 02:45:11 Run

After a bit of food and more congratulations, it was reward time! Rick and I headed straight for McDonalds and then returned to the beach for a muscle relieving walk in the cool water. With one easy meal, I managed to replace my entire sodium levels, courtesy of a cheeseburger combo. Then it was home for a shower, a well-deserved rest and a hard earned cold beer.

*Some people dream of success. Others wake up and achieve it.*
***Unknown***

# 18

# Party Time!

*Success should not leave you full, but hungry for more.*
*Susie O'Neill*

I am always keen for a party and after an achievement like finishing the HIM, I was ready to play! The drinks were going down well and I was buzzing with a variety of emotions that I had. One of the few regrets I have about finishing the HIM, was not asking enough of my friends how their race had gone. I was too consumed with celebrating my own success that I forgot to ask how their day was.

As the night continued, various people were acknowledged for the effort they had put in during the race. Luke McKenzie and Lisa Marangon were honoured as the respective professional winners, along with the age groupers and team placegetters. Brad Hosking, a West Australian fireman who ran the whole 21.1 km in complete fire fighting uniform with full breathing apparatus, was also acknowledged. Brad did this to raise money and awareness for the Tour of Duty run he was participating in with other fireman from around Australia and America. They were running from Los Angeles to New York, paying tribute to those lost in the September 11 terrorist attacks when the twin towers collapsed.

After this was done, I was called up on stage and presented with the Paul Goodman Award for completing the 2010 Busselton Half Ironman under courageous circumstances. This was a truly humbling, yet tremendous acknowledgment after the work I had put in to get myself to a condition where I could actually participate. It was very fitting to be standing in between Connie and Michael before the announcement was made, as these two in particular are probably among the few people around who really understand what the last 17 months had been like. Connie herself won the same award several years ago in her return to triathlon after surviving the 2002 Bali bombings; and Michael had broken his neck in a group cycling crash in 2007, before going on to complete multiple HIM and Ironman races in Busselton and Port Macquarie.

As I walked up to the stage, the crowd rose, led by the Busselton contingent to give me a standing ovation. My opening lines were not my best work – a simple 'Holy shit' which was received by even more applause. As I paused and turned to try to compose myself, the first name I saw on the shield was Connie, which I reminded the crowd of and got another boisterous cheer. The rest of the speech consisted of 'I'll keep this short, 18 months ago I was riding with Fabio, Mr Busselton, Mickey B and The Red Rocket, but if you don't know who they are it doesn't really matter. Special thanks to Jeff and Katie Greenfield from PhysioSouthWest who have been amazing with my rehabilitation……….'

I have no idea what else I said from there, but with the whole marquee listening to me, I didn't actually tell them how the accident happened; who the fab four were or anything about the recovery to get to where I was on that day. I still can't believe I didn't actually say those important things! I was definitely not looking in the direction of the Busselton crew, for I knew that I would lose it as soon as I saw any of them. But when I look back now, I really wish I had seen them. The big regret was not making more of the opportunity I had, but I do hate listening to speeches that drag on and on and having already put a few drinks away, I would not have been far from a rambling state.

I wish I had mentioned my Coach, Ross and how I was looking forward to having him train me again for an Ironman event and getting more pleasing results together. During my training for 2010, I often thought about the picture he drew for me of the glass half full. If the day and night I was having were anything to go by, it really was a great half!

Michael and Connie were the main instigators in nominating

## Party Time!

me for the award, and having a support base which includes special people like these has made the recovery a whole lot more bearable. There was another guy acknowledged just before I won, who had lost his wife to cancer. Also out on the course was a couple of blind competitors, as well as a man with only one arm. You see that and are instantly reminded that there is always someone else worse off than you and that if they can do it in that condition or with their circumstances, then a lot of healthy people who complain about their 'bad' race, or a 'crap' day or simply life in general, really need to ask themselves how bad things really are.

HIM and Ironman events are full of people who gave up and pulled out during the race for whatever reasons. Some get injuries that force them to withdraw, while others get injuries that they choose to let end their race. Some can handle it and are content with the decision, but I think and hope I will always have the fear of regret to keep me in the race until the end. In writing this book, I had been thinking about what the Paul Goodman Award means to me. I feel that there are three main things:

1. It is the delayed gratification for all the hard work I have done to get myself to the point where I could compete in the Half Ironman again.
2. It reminds me that the sport of triathlon is the best sport in the world.
3. Receiving this award was the best way of thanking and acknowledging everyone who has supported and helped me over the past 17 months.

Even though I had to go out and do the hard yards myself, the support I had from my fellow swimmers, riders and runners around town, through the Busselton Triathlon and Cycle Clubs was fantastic. Plenty of people helped me out a lot during training, but especially on the bike. It doesn't seem that long ago that I was getting a push up Alp de Cemetery (the very modest Cemetery Hill incline) most mornings. The people of Busselton had been very supportive as well. My association with The Busselton Jetty Swim, The Busselton Soccer Club and Geographe Bay Football Club added to the number of people who have encouraged me to keep working at getting fit again. I have some truly awesome friends here in Busselton and while my family lives back in New Zealand, I seem to be adopted by more and more families as the years go by.

So the rest and recovery could now begin, as I looked towards the 2011 HIM and hopefully another Ironman WA in the near future. But until then it was a very long and restful off season; sleeping in; watching some soccer; improving my cycling when my legs had recovered; working with my junior triathlon squad and enjoying a piece of cake or two. I do like cake!

*Adversity causes some men to break; others to break records.*
**William A Ward**

# 19

# Reality Bites!

*You have to expect things of yourself before you can do them.*
*Michael Jordan*

It was funny how many people around Busselton just presumed that I was doing the Ironman in 2010. The common question I would be asked was 'How's training going?' Sure, completing the HIM in May meant that I was on my way to completing an Ironman again, but I had a lot of fitness to get back and I needed to be sure that I was ready to do it – physically, but more importantly, mentally. A saving grace from the stress of worrying about entering the 2010 event was the decision to close entries midyear, as opposed to later in the year. While it had been very beneficial in previous years to train and then enter at the last minute, thus avoiding months of pressure, that was not an option anymore, due to the event's popularity and organisers publicising the event more around the world.

I knew back in February that I wouldn't be able to commit as early as June 30, and so it became easier to say an emphatic no, to anyone who asked if this was the goal I was aiming for. When entries became full before the end of April, I was the happiest person to have missed out. The next real goal was to go under 6 hours in the 2011 HIM and I knew I would need a year of training with plenty of recovery to do so. This began by doing very little through the month of May except reward myself with cake, icecream, the occasional beer and a few weeks of rest before hitting the gym and continuing on with the cycling.

As the weeks passed by towards race day, I became more relieved that I was not taking part. I was definitely not ready to be on a 16 – 20 week training program yet. Plus, I was on the waiting list for a further skin graft operation at the end of 2010, so I had to be sure that there would be no scheduled interruptions during the preparation. Ironman training is so hard on the body when you are fit, let alone damaged.

IMNZ in March 2011 was definitely on the radar at the beginning of 2010, but a lot would depend on how I went in the HIM in May. New Zealand would be a good location to return to, only having my family and a few friends to watch me and avoid the pressure of competing in Busselton. I wanted that pressure, but I wanted to be strong enough to handle it. So whilst I was confident after the HIM in May 2010, I did not want to do another Ironman and be out there for 15 or more hours. But even if New Zealand's event didn't go well, I would be surrounded by my family who would be happy just to see me, let alone participate in another Ironman and would not care about the result.

So New Zealand became the goal I was thinking more about. I told Ross, at the HIM Awards evening, but no one else. We would see how the off season went and whether I still had the desire when it came time to train. If not, IMWA at the end of 2011 was another option for me to consider.

IMNZ's popularity increased just as much as Ironman Australia at Port Macquarie and IMWA, here in Busselton. Entries were closing and would reach maximum capacity, which meant committing yourself financially for several months longer than we had to in earlier years. Having changed jobs in 2010 and the financial stresses that caused I didn't really have the money available at the time either, which was also a major factor for me to include in the thoughts I was having.

All of the signs were telling me that IMNZ 2011 wasn't going to happen. I couldn't afford the entry fee, or the flights across to New Zealand. These minor details could easily be overcome if necessary but thoughts of possible future surgery kept the doubts in my mind of having the hard work I had done in training, being

## Reality Bites!

undone by the unknown variables of operations and hospital stays. I was in no rush and knew the best solution was to wait until I had a few more factors in my favour, or at least within my control.

I have admiration and respect for anyone who takes on an Ironman, but get frustrated with people who want the glory, but aren't prepared to do any hard work to earn it. An Ironman can be achieved with very little training, provided you train smart, with quality, not necessarily quantity, and are willing to accept the finishing time you give yourself, which would reflect the amount of effort you put into your preparation. Above all else, I firmly believe that you need to respect the event itself and not take anything for granted, either beforehand, or on race day.

As the rest of 2010 went by, I accepted the fact that I just wasn't ready for such a long-term physical commitment to training. I could see that there would be financial, as well as the mental and physical stress of the Ironman and wasn't willing to take on the challenge at the moment. Also, I was not confident that my body would hold up over months of training. So I reassessed my priorities and did not enter IMNZ. Instead, I would continue trying to improve my cycling and strength building, aiming for a sub 6 hour time at the HIM in May 2011.

Having qualified as a Level 1 triathlon Coach in 2009, I had put together a squad of 6 junior athletes to train over the off season and through 2010 / 2011. I would use my rides with these young guns to keep building my fitness and gain a stronger base, for the HIM 2011.

*Sometimes it is not enough to do your best;
you have to do what's required.*
**Winston Churchill**

# 20

# Round 3

*Inside the ring or out, ain't nothing wrong with going down.
It's staying down that's wrong.*

**Cassius Clay**

The main reason why any future Ironman endeavours were put on hold was the regular assessments by both the Plastics and Orthopaedic Doctors of Royal Perth Hospital. In July 2010, Anthony Williams, my Plastic Surgeon advised that he was not happy with another area on my left leg and wanted to do another full thickness skin graft. I was on the waiting list and knew that it could happen anytime between then and the end of the year. The operation was scheduled for mid-November 2010 and had me back in hospital for 1 ½ weeks, not able to do very much. This would have made a serious dent in any training I had been doing for an Ironman in December, I felt certain of that. If not physically, then definitely mentally.

The lead up to any operation was usually always the same. Fast from midnight and only drink minimal amounts of water. From my room on the Ward, I was taken to the waiting area to begin the preparation for surgery, a place I was all too familiar with. This was a large room and could accommodate around 20 or so beds. I was wheeled in, along with my folder of medical notes which had grown throughout my time in hospital. Here, I would have a nurse come over and ask me my name; patient ID number; what I was having operated on; and what I was allergic to. Then they would leave and someone else would come over and ask the same or similar questions, such as what today's date was; what had happened to me, or other general questions. On the ceiling above each of the bed positions, were pictures of various landmarks around the world – Venice, Italy; Piccadilly Circus in London; The Colosseum in Rome to name a few. I guess these were designed to help the patients take their mind off surgery and not think about what lay ahead.

Then the surgeon would come in and say hello, followed by the Anaesthetist who always asked about allergies. Finally it was time to go through to theatre and I was wheeled down more corridors into the small operating room. Here, the surgery team were gathered - doctors, nurses, Anaesthetist and everyone else. They would explain what would happen and hook me up to the machines to monitor my vital signs. Finally the drugs would be injected and I would be out like a light, no matter how hard I tried to resist.

With each operation I would always try to count as high as I could before the anaesthetic took over. The trouble was that I could never remember what number I got up to or how long I had lasted, once the operation was over. I never had any problems with the anaesthetic or reactions to it, but on this occasion I did get a bit worried. When the needle was injected it seemed that the Anaesthetist released the fluid too quickly and I could feel the drug rushing through my veins and how cold it was. The tingling sensation increased and got stronger and stronger until it actually began to hurt. I must have been nearly at the knock out point, because as I expressed my concern to the medical team the lights when out and I was gone. There was obviously no problem afterward as I survived yet another operation, but I often think about that strange, intense feeling of such a cold liquid running through my arm. A feeling that is so weird, as it was inside the body, flowing through the bloodstream.

This was the only time that I could ever remember feeling uncomfortable or nervous about any operation, as the panic was occurring so close to surgery commencing. I doubt the medical team was worried at all, as once I was knocked-out, it didn't matter anymore.

# Round 3

All went well with this, my eleventh operation, and the only drawback was some stiffening of my left knee, along with the loss of general body strength.

*Don't be afraid to fail, because only through failure, do you learn to succeed.*
**Unknown**

## 21

# Not A One Hit Wonder

*If you don't invest very much, then defeat doesn't hurt very much and winning is not very exciting.*
### Dick Vermeil

While in hospital for the latest operation, entries opened for the HIM 2011 and were sold out within a few days. I had decided to enter, so that I didn't miss out and spent the rest of the year building up strength all over my body, ready to begin training on 01 January 2011. After the skin graft operation, the Orthopaedic doctors advised me that they wanted to do some keyhole surgery on my left knee to try and improve the bend and get more flexibility. This would only be possible once Plastics were satisfied that the skin was strong enough to handle this. The knee operation could be at any time, so I started training and would assess things once we had a better idea when the surgery would be. Hopefully after the HIM in May!

I volunteered and was a spectator at IMWA in December 2010, with entries opening for the 2011 race in mid-December. I was now beginning to have stronger thoughts of doing another Ironman, but was still content to wait until my body could handle the rigors of training and all operations were finished with. 2012 was the year I was now thinking about for a return to Ironman.

My 2011 HIM training was very similar to the 2010 training, as I couldn't start swimming until January, because of the recent skin graft operation and wasn't running again until I had built more strength in my knees and legs. Running was sore and awkward and I didn't enjoy it, so I didn't do it. I also believe that it is the main activity that will cause an injury, so I wanted to minimise it as much as possible. I hadn't ridden my bike for over a month, so it was almost back to the beginning again – or so it felt like! My goal for the 2011 HIM was to take about ½ hour off my time and finish with a sub 6 hours. I did a **05:58:08** hr. in 2007 and was trying to get somewhere close to this, maybe even better. That would have to mean a faster swim time and a much quicker bike time, knowing that I would not be able to improve the run time much, if at all. The 2010 HIM run was done with a constant pain that ran through my body with every step I took, but was masked by the euphoria and excitement of being out there again. The aching joints; lower back; hips and pelvis when I finished, however, were not hidden by anything.

I wrote myself an 18 week program, based similarly to 2010. I was soon at the pool doing lap after lap and riding regularly each week, building up the distance. Gym work continued and small runs of between 15 and 30 minutes began from Monday 03 January 2011. Week by week the distances increased until I was riding 100 km once a week with 2 shorter 40-50 km rides as well. Running was going okay, and was slowly building towards my longest distance of 15 km in about 100 minutes, with plenty of walking included in that time.

Gradually I saw myself getting fitter and losing a few kilograms along the way as well. The long slow rides were giving me a good base and the shorter, faster stuff was helping me get quicker. Things were coming together nicely. Slowly, but nicely! However, during my longest scheduled run of 110 minutes on Friday 08 April 2011, I had barely even begun and my whole body ached like never before. The slow jog became less than a brisk walk and I was soon hobbling towards home, finishing ten minutes shorter than I had planned to train for. My knees were aching, my lower back was killing me and my hips were very, very sore. The amount of training I was doing, particularly the running was taking its toll and my body was telling me so. That was the last run that I would do, I decided, convincing myself that based on last year's result of running nearly the whole way, I would be able to do the same again.

If I focused more on the swim and ride, I hoped that those two disciplines would be enough to get me through to the run with enough time to finish with a respectable result. I was still aiming for sub 6 hours, but wouldn't know if this was possible until the day arrived. Weather conditions would have to be favourable as well!

Saturday 07 May 2011 arrived and the Athletes with Disabilities got the race underway at 6:50 a.m. followed by the Pros and Open categories and then the Age Groupers. The 35–39 year old men's wave was the second last, leaving at 8:00 a.m. The South Westerly wind was just beginning to pick up and swimming 700 metres off shore was getting rather lumpy. As has nearly always been the case, with prerace nerves and excitement, I didn't start my Heart Rate Monitor and stop watch, so finished the swim not knowing for sure what my time was. I was aiming for less than 40 minutes this year, so figured I would have been around that, as I had a fair idea of how fast I could swim. Through transition and over to my bike, it was the usual process of breathing slowly, trying to drop the heart rate, while getting shoes, socks and helmet on, washing the salt water out of my mouth and getting the first pieces of food in to me.

The wind was tough on the way out and was only going to get worse. Slowly the speed started to climb. It felt like I was only doing about 20 kmph at the start and I was desperately trying to get up to 30 kmph. There were not many places that gave a tail wind in the first half of the lap, so surely it would have to be easier coming back to town. Yes, it was, but not as much as everyone was hoping for and the weaker riders were really starting to suffer. It felt like there was only between 5 km and 10 km of each lap that the wind really gave you some decent assistance. This was probably my worst ride for nutrition that I had ever had, and I have had a few! The protein bars I ate tasted like cardboard on this occasion and I struggled to finish one and keep it down. I didn't even drink one whole bottle of electrolyte and only got one carbohydrate gel into me. Nothing was staying down and I finished the bike knowing I had not eaten anything close to what I should have. This year's nutrition was way worse than last year.

Due to the wave starts being over an hour from first to last, as

## A Long Ride Back

we were heading out for our first lap of the bike, most of the first wave competitors were either flying past on their second lap, or heading home to begin the run. And then as we were beginning the second lap of the bike, the starting athletes were running towards us on their second lap of the run. Their day was nearly over and I was only halfway through the bike leg! A computer malfunction with my speedometer meant that I had no idea of my ride time, but knew it wasn't even close to the 2:30 hr. I was aiming for. Hopefully it was around last years' time of 2:45 hr. so I wouldn't be too far behind where I wanted to be.

Finally, the 90 km was over and it was through transition for the second time. Bike shoes and helmet off, running shoes on and out to the run course. It was a lovely sunny day and the temperature was rising to the high 20's. The wind was still steady, but not as bad as trying to ride into it. The run began and the stomach cramps arrived shortly after. Within the first 1 km I was desperate for a toilet. An evacuation was imminent and the toilet block didn't seem to be getting any closer. Unfortunately it was already occupied, so I carried on, focusing on the green port-a-loo at the first aid station. I could have screamed when this was in use as well, but luckily it was a short wait and I carried out a very swift withdrawal.

Back onto the run and the plan was to eat the biscuits at the aid station, to get some solid food into my stomach. But the biscuits were nowhere to be seen. I had to drink to keep cool and hydrated, but the liquid sitting in my stomach just gave me the stitch. On the way back to finish the first lap, the stomach cramps were back and another toilet stop produced nothing, but it sure didn't feel like that when I ran! Eventually the halfway point arrived. My Heart Rate Monitor was annoying me and my Fuel Belt carrying my water seemed to be weighing me down. As I ran past my support team, I dropped them both to the ground and carried on, feeling freer and lighter instantly. Luckily I didn't get busted for outside assistance. I was downing the coke on the aid stations and the sugar buzz was working well. But the ride had exhausted me and I was walking far too much. My body wasn't very sore and there was no pain from my knees, hips or back, like I had in training or last year. I was simply too tired to run. Finally, the last 3.5 km was there and I was willing myself to the finish. I was playing leap frog with Troy Buswell, a local Member of Parliament, who was running in a team. The competitiveness that all athletes have took over and I decided that I had to beat him to the finish line. Not a big accomplishment, but pride is a funny thing sometimes. One by one the markers were ticked off – The party houses with support music blaring; the Higgins' house; the last aid station; the Watson's house; the Marine Sea Rescue Building; and after what seemed like an eternity, the line of support tents with Michael, Scott Wilson and a few others cheering everybody along.

Finally, the finish chute was in sight and the sprint to the line meant the day was finally over. The final time:

**HIM 2011** – Total - **06:23:00**
00:40:31 Swim / 02:54:48 Bike / 02:40:15 Run

It was nowhere near the **05:57:00** I was aiming for, but it was a couple of minutes quicker than 2010. At least I hadn't got slower! I couldn't believe it took me nearly 3 hours on the bike and yet my run time was 5 minutes quicker than last year! I had trained so well for the bike and had cut my running back to nothing in the final month. It's funny how all the preparation and training you do is often in vain. If things don't come together on the day, there is nothing much that you can do about it. As Ross would say – 'That's triathlon!'

The more I thought about it afterwards, the more I realised how much pressure I had put on myself to finish under 6 hours. The 2010 result would have been great regardless of the time, as it was my first event back since the crash. Now, being a year ahead, I was expecting a lot more from myself to get the result, that I forgot about relaxing, having fun and just enjoying being out there. I was trying to do positive things like ride harder and run faster, but was constantly telling myself mentally that I couldn't; it was too hard; I wasn't strong enough and I needed to slow down and walk. A tough lesson to learn sometimes and one that seems to recur all through my life, regardless of the situation!

## A Long Ride Back

So with the last race of the season over, it was time to catch up with my fellow competitors to see how their race went and have a well-earned beer or two. Not having to train as much meant enjoying my sleeping in a lot more as well!

The awards presentations and after party followed the HIM, later that night and I was eager to see who the winner of the Paul Goodman award for this year would be. Jeremy McClure, a blind athlete competing in his first ever triathlon, let alone HIM, was given the honour, much to everyone's approval. Jeremy's time was just over 5 hours, an unbelievable result with very impressive splits.

After my last doctor's consultation, a few weeks after race day, I was advised that the operation on my knee was planned for late 2011, which would have once again hampered any training progress for the Ironman, if I had entered. This confirmed that my decision not to enter IMWA in 2011 was the right one. I just hoped that this would be the last of the surgeries and I could put all of my hospital visits behind me.

I had been for regular appointments with both Plastics and Orthopaedic doctors over the past 2 ½ years, checking to see how everything was going. Orthopaedics were not going to do anything until Plastics had finished their work with my skin grafts. They were keen to redo a couple of areas on my leg that they were still not happy with, but I wanted to wait and give Orthopaedics a chance to try and improve my leg flexion in the hope that it would bend more than it was currently.

So the middle part of 2011 was spent riding to help train the juniors and adults I was coaching and also for my own physical fitness. The other goal that developed over the second half of the year was getting serious about the writing of this book.

Llando Pyke, another friend from New Zealand, now living here as my flatmate in Busselton, had entered IMWA 2011 for the first time. Aidan had signed up as well, so I began coaching both of them throughout the year in the lead up to the December event. I had only been training juniors at this stage, so was looking forward to working with adults for a big event and watching their progress on race day.

> *When an archer misses the mark, he turns and looks for the fault within himself. Failure to hit the bull's-eye is never the fault of the target. To improve your aim – improve yourself.*
> **Gilbert Arland**

*Back on the bike and in the zone! Busselton's HIM 2010 and it's just like old times.*

*Photo Credit – Leonie Paine*

*Apparently I'm running! I'm about to leave Katie Greenfield in my dust – yeah right! I've just been "chicked" as Katie laps me during HIM 2010, but getting both of us in the same shot makes this a very special photo!*

*Photo Credit - Marathon Photos*

*Congratulations from my friends after finishing the HIM 2010, as they make sure I stay upright! This photo highlights the difference in the size of my thighs.*

*Photo Credit – Belinda Higgins*

*Sharing a well-earned drink with Michael Bray and Connie Watson at the Awards night!*

*Photo Credit – Cate Finlay*

*Holding the 2010 Paul Goodman Award Shield after my composed and eloquent speech!*

*Photo Credit – Cate Finlay*

*The Paul Goodman Award Trophy that I get to keep. Very cool indeed!*

*Photo Credit – Steve Crenfeldt*

*The run leg of Busselton's HIM 2011. Another race day nearly over.*
*Photo Credit – Leonie Paine*

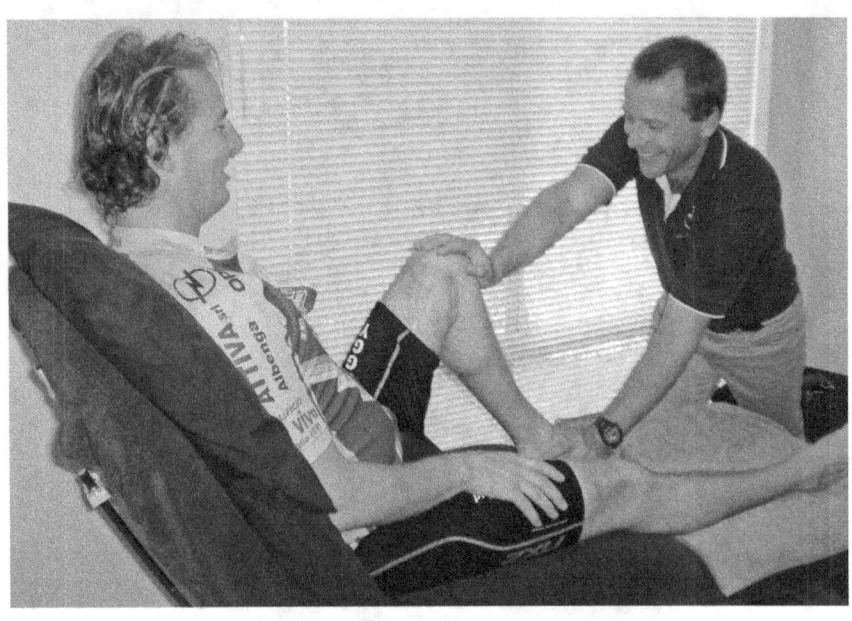

*Jeff Greenfield working on my knee, more than 3 years after the accident. He was always the one who was smiling for some reason!*
*Photo Credit – Steve Crenfeldt*

*Me and my Coach, Ross Pedlow from Exceed Triathlon Club in January 2012. Ross's hospitality ensures any Busselton athletes are warmly welcomed to their tent before and after a race, especially the Tuff-n-up crew!*

*Photo Credit – Carolyn Baker*

# 22

# Negative Gearing

*Our greatest weakness lies in giving up. The most certain way to succeed is to always try something one more time.*
**Thomas Edison**

Before the accident, I was not entirely happy with my life. Most days felt like I wasn't even really living anymore, I was simply in a daily rut, almost a Ground Hog Day, where nothing seemed to be worth doing. Sure, I would enjoy parts of every day, but the majority of my time seemed to be a waste. I didn't see my job at Carpet Choice as what I wanted to be doing forever, but I had no idea of what I did want.

After doing some sports journalism for The Busselton-Dunsborough Mail in 2008, a lot of people told me I should consider this as a career. Writing sports articles for soccer and footy made me realise however, that even though I enjoy writing, I wouldn't want that as a job. Writing about topics I did not relate to and the time management required to reach deadlines would have seen me lose this passion, I feel certain about that. I get pleasure from writing about the things that I want to write, not from what I have to write.

If you know anything about the temperaments and traits associated with people's personalities, there are four main types:

Choleric – you want things done your way and right now.
Melancholy – you like things done correctly and in proper order.
Sanguine – you like things to be fun and social.
Phlegmatic – you like to relax and value peacefulness.

## A Long Ride Back

My personality is generally fairly relaxed and laid back, which makes being Phlegmatic as my dominate temperament. This is closely followed by Melancholy, as I like to make lists and spend lots of time getting things 'just right' before actually doing what needs to be done. I have a handful of Sanguine traits, so I like to have fun and focus on the social side of things, not seeing the hard work involved in many tasks. With very little Choleric characteristics I don't like to lead, take charge or demonstrate assertiveness.

So I would describe myself as a relaxed, easy going procrastinator who thinks too much about what needs to be done and would rather be off having fun than actually doing the work involved. I am pretty happy most of the time and even though I enjoy socialising and hanging out with my friends as often as I can, I am also quite comfortable by myself. I like to think that I am positive most of the time, and try to find the positives in most things. I enjoy watching movies and reading stories about overcoming difficulties and when the underdog triumphs and accomplishes something big. However, when I would try to relate the 'big' thing to something that I would think of doing or accomplishing, my self-doubt would instantly shut down these positive thoughts and I would tell myself that 'you couldn't do that, so don't kid yourself that you think you can'.

The negative self-talk that we give to ourselves is often constant and continuous, regardless of how positive we try to be. In fact, we are often our own worst enemy and biggest critic, when it comes to accomplishing dreams and goals. I am definitely no exception. In fact, I am probably the best (or worst) there is.

So I was occupying my time to try and help keep myself positive and having goals like the HIM and Ironman to work towards were very beneficial. But no matter how hard I tried, my attitude was dropping and I was becoming increasingly negative. I didn't like that and I could see and feel myself heading further downhill. So as the saying goes – If you want to change some things in your life, you have to change some things in your life!

I was trying to read every day for around 15 minutes, books

## Negative Gearing

which were educational; biographical or just generally positive, to work on improving the attitude I had but I would always leave this until the last thing at night and be too tired to do it or put it off, knowing I had to be up early in the morning to exercise. What I really mean here is that I would waste away the evening by either surfing the net; reading the rubbish that is written on Facebook (and adding to it); or resort to the comfort of the idiot box – TV, all the time worrying about what I should be doing instead of these worthless activities. I had plenty of more constructive things I could have been undertaking, that's for sure!

The same feelings existed in 2006 when I began training for my first Ironman, as I entertained the thoughts of being good enough to be in the top twenty finishers of my age group. Again, the self-talk would shut these ideas down and I would return to simply training to complete the event and that would be enough. My finishing times at races would confirm that I was so far off the pace that that was never going to happen. As a result, I would then be content to just take part, cross the finish line and enjoy the moment.

So throughout my training, I would ride within my limits, while still hoping somehow, that the training I was doing was enough to get a faster time on the day. All I wanted was to have trained well enough to be satisfied with the result I achieved. If I did the hard work in training, then I would improve and have a finishing time that I could be happy with. This continued most of the time and along with the coaching assistance from Ross, as well as reading positive material, I began to focus on my training for the 2007 / 2008 season. This worked well for IMNZ in March 2008 and the Busselton HIM in May 2008. I was trying to continue this positive attitude and self-belief into the 2008 / 2009 season…right up until the day of the crash.

*It is in your moments of decision that your destiny is shaped.*
***Anthony Robbins***

# 23

# Mental And Physical Traction

*Whatever the mind can conceive and believe the mind can achieve.*
*Jean-Napoleon Hill*

As I lay in the hospital bed of RPH, unable to move very much, I thought that a positive attitude was required to assist my recovery. However, being positive in hospital was not really that hard, as I quickly realised that it was more patience and time that was required, than anything else. I just had to wait until I was mobile again so that I could then utilise a positive attitude. Little did I know how long I would have to keep it going for! Ironically, I actually began getting annoyed with people who told me to stay positive and think positive, because I felt that it wasn't necessary or possible so early on.

Without my steady stream of visitors each day, I would have struggled with my situation massively, I feel certain about that. Having my friends come to see me and take my mind off the boring, mundane, routine of life in a hospital bed, was my saviour. It was about just getting through the days until the traction came off. Eat, bath, exercise, sleep, eat, exercise, sleep, and eat – all from the bed I lay in and often from an angle of only 30 degrees. It was still not as bad as what other people had to go through, but it was still crap.

Everyone would tell me how lucky I was and still do over 3 years later. It is such a funny thing to say when you think about it:

I was lucky that the truck didn't run over me.
I was lucky that it was only my lower body that was injured.
I was lucky that I only broke one foot, not two.

## A Long Ride Back

I was lucky that my spinal cords were missed and I had no damage to my head and neck.

I was lucky that I only needed skin grafts on one leg, not two.

Lucky. Stuck in a hospital bed; on my back for 10-12 weeks; often unable to move my lower body more than a few centimetres without sending waves of pain through my body. Yip, I'm lucky! Lucky to be alive, I know, but I can't help thinking that if I was luckier, then none of this would have happened at all.

I never heard a single thing from APH Construction, or the driver of the truck who hit me. Not even a phone call to someone, to find out how I was doing (that I was aware of). Whether this was for legal reasons, I don't know. Maybe it would have been seen as admitting fault or liability or something. Not hearing anything from them really annoyed me and still does today. No phone call, no flowers, no card, nothing. To me that is just wrong. It seemed common courtesy to make some form of contact, surely. He didn't have to admit fault or even apologise, but it would have been nice to know that someone had at least enquired about me.

I even wrote out a letter to APH Construction myself, explaining how things happened from my side to try and get some answers as to what the driver saw and did but during a phone call to Michael one day, he talked me out of sending it and now, I am glad that he did. Why should I have been the one to contact them, when they couldn't do the same for me? Apparently the driver moved up north to work in the mines, so I heard from a few people around town. Sometimes I wondered whether he was emotionally scarred from what happened. I'm sure it must have been hard for him too, but I guess he got over it easily enough.

As the drug dependence slowly decreased, I had more time and clearer thoughts to analyse the accident's consequences. Clipping Michael's wheel was one thing. I still could have fallen off, got a few scratches, grazes, maybe a broken bone or two and probably done some damage to my bike. The lads would have come back, made sure I was okay and then told me 'get up you girl's blouse' or

## Mental And Physical Traction

'Tuff-n-Up Princess' and I would have limped back into town feeling sorry for myself. To me that would have been the worst of the best case scenario. If it had simply been a couple of bikes getting tangled up, then I could handle living with the knowledge that it was my own fault and that would be the end of it, but as far as I was concerned, the truck driver was following too close behind us, regardless of what anyone says.

Many people had begun asking me if I would ride again. Some days, while in Shenton Park, I would think yes. Other days, it was a definite no. I thought I would, but to what extent, I was never sure. I felt like I had to prove something to others more than to myself. And I also think that I needed to repay everyone for the support they were showing me, by riding, or even doing triathlons again. At this time I was never sure, but thankfully, it was such a long way into the future that the decision didn't need to be made immediately.

Whenever Ross came to visit, we would inevitably talk about this topic and he always told me that I would ride again. He also said that I didn't have to, but he believed I would. He also told me that I would do another triathlon. I still wasn't so sure.

Once I was back riding my bike, people asked if I was worried about having another accident on any level or get scared when I'm out riding. The night before I ride, I often find myself lying in bed nervous and anxious of going out the next day. Obviously I am not crippled by this fear, but I often think about something similar happening again, to either me or someone else.

I'm often asked if I still think about what happened during the accident or if I remember the details. I was conscious for the whole time, but there are parts I just don't recall, or am not sure of. I believe this is for a reason and not knowing doesn't really matter. The answer to the first question is yes, I think about it every day, usually several times a day. I think it's impossible not to when you have to look at the result every morning in the shower.

I've asked myself the 'why' question countless times and am no closer to answering it. I don't know why this had to happen to me or why the truck had to try and pass us on that part of the road. I'm sure there is a reason, but I haven't found it yet. When I read books about people overcoming adversity and trouble in their lives, they usually go on to do something amazing or miraculous.

Maybe this is yet to come for me. Or, maybe the reason was for someone else's benefit and has served their purpose and I didn't need to know about it. Or maybe it's still to come for them and me. Or, maybe I have missed the lesson and the purpose all together! I don't know. I still don't know what good has come out of the whole ordeal.

What I do know is that a lot of the time, my life still feels like it did before the accident. I still don't think I am any closer to finding out what the lesson was, or why I wasn't more seriously injured or even killed. I guess all I can do is hope that it will be revealed to me one day. I'd like that.

*We can either watch life from the sidelines, or actively participate…Either we let self-doubt and feelings of inadequacy prevent us from realizing our potential, or embrace the fact that when we turn our attention away from ourselves, our potential is limitless.*
**Christopher Reeve**

# 24

# Going Through The Motions

*Faith is the daring of the soul to go further than it can see.*
**William Newton Clarke**

At the time of the accident, I was going out with a lovely lady, who had been by my side for nearly all of my time in hospital. Peta travelled up to Perth, from Busselton, as often as possible, taking time off work and doing everything she could think of to be positive for me. We had been together since June 2008 and things were going quite well for us both. But once I was out of hospital and my rehabilitation really began, my priority became more about me and less about her. I was not dealing with a number of things and was reaching breaking point. I had only been home a month; was still heavily reliant on drugs and painkillers; was trying to assist with daily dressing changes on my body; had to see my legs in close detail all of the time; was trying to become independent again and was right into daily physiotherapy. Not that I want these to sound like excuses, but I was struggling to handle everything myself and wasn't reaching out for help like I should have. Peta is an immensely positive person, yet the more positive she was on my behalf, the more this added to my frustration.

Despite getting out of hospital in January 2009 and beginning my life again, I was still in a very dark place myself. A couple of notes I had made during my recovery were about how 'if my body aches this much now, then how much worse will it get?' Another one, was asking myself 'whether I could afford mentally and financially to carry on through the rehabilitation process', that had no end in sight. I was also still coming to terms with how my leg looked; the physical difference I now had; always being reminded of and having to answer questions about the crash; and what my life would be like from now on. These were feelings I would have for months and years to come.

I was slowly becoming more mobile, but was still requiring a lot of help. This began to infuriate me, that I couldn't do everything for myself, like I used to. My frustrations were being taken out on Peta and I hated myself for the way things were going, how I was behaving and what I was saying. It was only going to get worse and the only solution I could see was to end the relationship. So I did. Not my best work and looking back I wish I had handled things better but I had become so self-centred that even though Peta was being incredibly supportive, caring, loving and giving, I didn't want it. Looking back, this was the right decision to make at the time, but it definitely wasn't an easy one. It was painful and difficult and I felt extremely low, mean even, to be so self-centred and selfish. I wanted my life to go back to how it was before, when I had more control over things and we were both happier.

Several weeks passed with some interesting conversations between Peta and I and then we didn't see or speak to each other for a while, mainly because we weren't going to the same places, even though we still had a similar circle of friends. Luckily though, time is a bit of a healer, as they say, and over the years we have become friends again and I am frequently reminded of how supportive, caring and loving Peta was during those dark times, not that I will ever forget.

As the recovery and rehabilitation intensified now was the time that I required the positive attitude. I needed to keep repeating the same boring and mundane exercises each day to get my body stronger. The results were so slow and insignificant to me that I would often think that there was no point in continuing, so I might as well give up. And giving up had a wide variety of meanings, most of which I entertained in my mind at some point over the past few years.

I was trying to get my life back to the way it was – which ironically, I didn't like. Eventually I was back doing most of the things I could do before, just slower or with some difficulty; but my spare time was not being used as productively as it could be. My reliance on drugs faded away and I was soon medication free, but wasn't able to handle full time employment yet. I was in a unique position, where I had the time to do things, but not the cash flow to support me. It didn't take long for the money to run low, when there was no consistent income for a few weeks, but still bills to be paid, during the times when insurance paperwork was being completed and processed.

My life had become a constant whirlwind of activity throughout 2009 and into 2010, as I tried to do ten things at once, but often not accomplishing anything substantial whenever I set out to do it. Being fairly disorganised wasn't helping the situation either! I needed to prioritise the important things, drop the ones I was either sick of doing or wanted a change from; and most importantly, not take on anything else! What's that saying? – 'The man, who chases two rabbits, will catch neither'.

I had thought about cutting back on commitments in other years, but by the end of 2010, I was becoming so mentally exhausted that I needed to focus on a few things and really try to do them well and forget about the rest. What I had to accept was, that other people could do what I was doing, just as well as me; and that if I stopped doing these things and they were important enough, someone else would choose to do them. With that, I also had to stop procrastinating in order to accomplish more of the things I was trying to achieve.

So through the recovery of the past 3 years since the accident, I have been trying to occupy my time with constructive activity and positive thoughts, even though there are still plenty of times where I have the same negative thoughts about how my life is going. Sometimes my attitude would rise and fall every hour, or even more frequently. I could be up and down and up and down within minutes or even seconds of each other as positive thoughts were immediately counteracted by negative thoughts and so on. I tried to find balance in my life, with friends; work; relationships; family;

money and exercise; as well as working on my dreams and goals, one of which had become writing and publishing this book. Most days are a battle within myself as I try to remain positive with all of the things I do. It is shocking how negative we can be to ourselves and how positive we are to other people, when it is ourselves who need the positive energy and attitude.

As I tried to improve and maintain my fitness, there were many minor setbacks that had me testing my positive attitude, such as getting a cold over winter; feeling tired and unfit on group rides and not being able to keep up. Questioning whether I wanted to stay in bed or get up and exercise; right through to knowing that another operation was scheduled and I would lose whatever fitness I had and have to start again. These things, along with the frustrations of not achieving the tasks I would set myself, would have me rising and falling every day, through the ups and downs of life. Life seemed to return to a daily existence of exercise, rehabilitation, eat, work and sleep, on a continuous, repetitive cycle. Once the physiotherapy ended, training took its place, and what once was hard work but fun became a tedious chore due to the limitations of my body.

From early on in the physiotherapy practice and seeing how little my leg bent, I had resigned myself to not being able to work full time again, in a physical capacity. Over time, this has changed, but there are plenty of actions I have to do differently now, to compensate. Simple things that most people take for granted are still very uncomfortable for me – climbing ladders and stairs; getting in and out of cars; sitting in confined spaces where I have to keep my leg at the same angle for long periods of time; squatting or kneeling; sitting down on the floor and standing up again and stepping over things all have to be done in a way to allow for my leg not bending like it should naturally. Again, these are just examples of things I could do before without a hassle, but now are just annoying, frustrating and often painful. How I long for the day when I can bend my left leg as much as my right leg. Then I might feel like I have made a full recovery.

Then there are still the physical scars that I am faced with every day. Having to look in the mirror and see my leg in the condition it is in, brings a variety of thoughts and feelings. It is incredible what the plastic surgeons could do to get my leg as good as they have, but it is also one of the most unattractive things I have seen. I still worry what any future partners will think when they see it. It's not too bad when you only see some of it, but knowing it goes all the way up to my waist and right around, is not an appealing thought. It is still something that I am very self-conscious of and I have become very fast and stealth like, at getting dressed, whenever I am out in public. Often comments are made or a question is asked by onlookers about what happened. When I mention that it was a pushbike, not a motorbike, like they have presumed, I've even had looks of disbelief as though I am lying. That really annoys me!

My left leg will always be thinner than my right leg, and building up the muscle will never bring both legs back to the same size. The fat layer which was ripped off will not return, leaving a definitive difference on my body. With most of the nerves gone as well, I cannot feel hot or cold temperatures when items are placed on my leg, but strangely enough, this is always warmer than any other part of my body. With no hair follicles to grow either, I only have to shave 1 ½ legs for race day!

Not long after the 2010 HIM, I began a new relationship with a lady named Rosemary, who I met through friends associated with soccer and triathlon, in Busselton. Rosemary is a positive, vibrant and wonderful lady, with an infectious smile, which is always on display. Rosemary accepted me as I was, unconditionally, with scars and all, setting aside most of my self-conscious concerns. Even though I had this terrific lady to enjoy life with again, I still wasn't happy with myself and as a consequence, our relationship didn't last, despite the best efforts to make things work. We had a magnificent year together, which included her supporting me through my third visit to RPH for further surgery as well as the HIM 2011 and I am very fortunate to have been able to share a portion of my life with this fantastic lady.

## A Long Ride Back

A common question that I am still asked even today is 'is everything back to normal now, since your accident'. I never quite know how to answer that and always have to pause and take a breath to stop me from replying to a fairly innocent question, in a reactive and rude way. I usually just say 'Yes, everything is fine' or 'Yeah, as good as it can be' or 'Yes, everything is going great, thanks'. I don't like dwelling on my situation and telling people the details of exactly how I feel is not what anyone wants, or needs to hear. Then I try to change the subject and hope that that is the end of it. Sometimes this works, sometimes it doesn't. I still do not enjoy talking about the accident, or the recovery, which is ironic that I decided to write a book about it. Maybe it's to tell people what they are too afraid to ask. I don't know.

One thing that always floored me during my rehabilitation and I still hear it today, is the comment made by a wide variety of people, including medical professionals who thought that the problem with my leg was that it didn't straighten, as opposed to bend. First of all, it had to remain straight, in traction for 12 or so weeks, so surely that was an indication that straightening wasn't the issue. Secondly, if I had a leg that remained bent and could not straighten, then how on earth could I walk properly, let alone run or ride a bike? I guess hearing these comments was magnified by my feeling that one of the biggest issues and physical challenges I had, which seemed so obvious and was well documented, was not grasped by people who either had to look through my medical file and history before seeing me, or were 'following' my progress, but not as closely as it looked.

As I returned to cycling, I became a lot more cautious when I rode, probably too much in fact and have slowly developed a lot more confidence now, than in the early months when I began again. I soon realised however, that there are so many circumstances out of your control that can affect you, no matter how careful you are. I've had near misses since the accident, with cars; other riders; hazards on the road; animals and even the odd truck that has flown past at 100 kmph and didn't give me any room when doing so. Just as drivers do the wrong thing though sometimes, cyclists do too. Some riders do not wear helmets all the time, and many ride without wearing anything bright or reflective on their clothing. Others do not even have lights on when they ride in the dark. However, impatient drivers who pass cyclists on blind corners, or stay as close as they can while overtaking, are just idiots. In hindsight, we should have reported these instances to the police more often, but the cyclist is usually trying to stay upright, and isn't focusing on the registration plate or description of the vehicle as it speeds past. There is also the fear of retribution that may take place and cars travelling twice or three times faster than you generally disappear into the distance. More often than not, most cyclists are only saved by pure luck. (There's that word again).

These few bad times, do not compare with the countless good times I have when I ride though. The camaraderie; the atmosphere; the socialising afterwards; the shitty feeling of getting dropped when you can't keep up; and the naughty feeling of dropping others when you are feeling strong, are all reasons why I will continue to ride, hopefully for a long time to come. I may never be as strong as the other guys in town and I still ride within my limits, not pushing myself enough when it gets hard, but as long as I am still enjoying it, then that is all that matters to me.

Even though I was back cycling and had made a successful return to triathlon, I was still not satisfied. Despite all of the positive reinforcements; you-can-do-it's; make the most of your second chance at life; I was yet to find anything that got me so fired up to accomplish something really significant. When you don't know what you want or what you are supposed to do with your life, then merely existing doesn't really seem that exciting. I was finding it worse having come so close to dying; I didn't understand why I wasn't more excited about living! You hear and see stories about people who have tragedy strike them and they go on to accomplish amazing things. I wanted to have a successful life and do that too, but I didn't know what it was that I wanted. I was looking for things that stimulate and motivate me; that give me passion; that make life exciting. Things that keep me awake at

## A Long Ride Back

night and get me out of bed early. But just like the song by U2 – I still haven't found what I'm looking for…

*If you want to be enthusiastic, act enthusiastic.*
*Inner enthusiasm follows.*
**William Ellis**

# 25

# The Positivity Chapter - Eventually

*Believe in yourself. You must do that which
you think you cannot.*
**Eleanor Roosevelt**

A few people had made the suggestion to me, fairly early on, that I should write a book about what happened. I had dismissed this idea initially, but over time, I began to think about the progress I had made and the initial notes I had gathered, when keeping my friends and family updated through email. So I began writing. This gave me something to occupy my spare time and could be done at my own pace, without any pressure, especially as no one knew about it until it was close to being finished. When the rough versions were ready, they were proofread by several key people who told me whether it was worth pursuing or not. I guess, if you're reading this, then enough people thought it was!

When I think back to when the crash happened and more specifically why it happened, I guess the one thing that I wanted to come from my accident, was that I would be changed from what I was beforehand to something better. It's as though I wanted it to be like I was struck by lightning and from that moment, I'd be more confident, organised, assertive, fired up, disciplined and focused, which would make me overcome all of my fears and struggles and lead me to the success of accomplishing everything I wanted. When I think of other successful people, they seem to have had something similar and an epiphany follows. From that point on, they went out and conquered the world and nothing was going to stop them. Why didn't I have that and why wasn't I doing that?

What I feel I have learned however, is that this doesn't ever happen. Sure the lightning strike and the epiphany does, but from then on the goal is set and the plan, action and steps are put in place to achieve it, along with developing an attitude to want to accomplish the goals. I think it's like writing this book. I could never have sat down and written this thing solid from start to finish. Life happens and I have to stop to eat, sleep, work and so on, but the plan was to do something every day to reach the goal of finishing it - kind of like being on a triathlon training program. It started with a few words, which turned into a page, then a chapter. Notes were made, research was done, and questions were asked. Timing goals weren't always reached and are quite laughable when I look back at them, but I knew that if I was consistent and persistent and did a little bit at a time, the end result would come.

Ross planted another seed by suggesting I become a triathlon coach myself. This was around 2009, at the stage when we didn't know if I would ever be able to participate in events again. He knew I enjoyed the sport enough to want to stay involved in some way. Gaining qualification and forming a small squad of juniors soon followed. This became however, another thing I was doing in my already limited spare time.

Volunteering to assist on committees was just one of the traits that I got from my parents. I was the Secretary of The Busselton Cycle Club for a number of years and am also on the committees of The Busselton Jetty Swim and The Busselton Triathlon Club. Each of these roles holds different responsibilities and has their own share of time consuming tasks, big and small. Include my job and training for the Half Ironman as well as looking at other business and employment opportunities over the past few years, as well as starting a new relationship and you can see how I was throwing myself into lots of different things to keep busy and not dwell on the accident, but was becoming so frustrated that I didn't have enough time to do what I wanted….and I still didn't know what that was!

So at the beginning of 2011, I resigned as Secretary of The Busselton Cycle Club. This was counteracted however, by taking on the Vice President's role on the Busselton Triathlon Club a few

## The Positivity Chapter - Eventually

months earlier, as we tried to keep the club alive and active in town. Unfortunately, for the host town of the two biggest triathlons in Western Australia, the club itself has often struggled with internal support, even though more and more local athletes take part each year. Now, in the middle of the 2011 / 2012 season, our club is in a much stronger position than it was a year ago and I was able to stand down as Vice President, with Max taking over the role for the year.

One rewarding position I did have during the 2010 / 2011 season was running the kids Trystars programme in Busselton. This was however, adding to my frustration, using my spare time to teach children the basic fundamentals of triathlon. The weeks went on and it often felt like I was wasting my time writing session plans and meeting them each week. The kids were often not listening or paying attention. It seemed like they were uninterested and weren't really trying, no matter what I tried to do to keep things fun and enjoyable. Towards the end of the season, during a few club events and the Kids Triathlon at the Half Ironman, I was pleasantly surprised to see them taking part, having fun, smiling and doing really well. The basics had sunken in somewhere along the way and the hard work had paid off, with the kids showing off their excitement at the new skills they had developed, proving to all of us that they had actually learned something, while having fun at the same time. Needless to say their parents and I were very pleased with this outcome.

This turned out to be very satisfying and was a great example of delayed gratification, especially seeing the kid's enthusiasm about wanting to do Trystars again next year. As the 2011 / 2012 season began, I took on the role of running this program again, and with a few other people offering to assist me, I felt that this will be beneficial for everyone – the parents, the organisers and especially the kids. I still had a few of my juniors, along with a couple of adults to coach as well, so I know that I will still be involved in the sport of triathlon, even though I am taking the entire season off to give my body a rest. But I need to stay on The Busselton Jetty Swim Committee, because Jenny won't let me leave yet!

## A Long Ride Back

Through writing my story, I think I have found my dream and my passion and my purpose. Writing has always been my passion, a lot of people would agree with that. My dream has become this book. To write it and publish it and sell hundreds of copies so that people will read it and become inspired to set their own dreams and goals to reach, whatever they are, big or small. If only one person does that, then helping one person is fine with me. If one person sees themselves as average and then sets out to do something that they don't think they can do, and their belief builds over time until they reach their goal, then I believe my story was worth telling.

My goal is to sell 2000 copies within the first 6 months of its release and enable me to donate significant portions of the proceeds to the charities and causes which are important to me. It is a big goal! But surely 2000 books, in countries of millions, has to be possible. So when someone asks if they can borrow your copy, tell them they have to buy their own, please!

I am a big fan of the Pay It Forward principal and philanthropy of all levels. Experiencing firsthand how much help and support I received has given me a few ideas of what I can do to enrich other people's lives and I look forward to trying to implement these in the future.

I had set myself a number of smaller goals during 2011. The first was to not eat McDonald's; KFC or Hungry Jacks for over a year, which started on Tuesday 09 November 2010 and has lasted well into 2012. I even planned on having it for my birthday in February, but didn't really feel the urge! Now don't assume that I have become a massive health freak by this decision, as I have still eaten a lot of rubbish through this time frame - just ask the guys at work! The goal was more the challenge to see if I could do it.

The second goal is to read every single day. This has either been a chapter or several pages from a book, for around 15 minutes. Sometimes it is longer, other times, I have only managed a page or two. But the point is that I have kept the goal going and developed the habit, which I am determined not to break for a while yet.

## The Positivity Chapter - Eventually

Another goal was to finish this book by 31 July 2011. This moved to 31 August and then on to 31 October, as more information was added each time I opened it and reread it. Then the goal moved to being published before Christmas 2011, but that quickly disappeared with the chaos and mayhem of the end of year rush. Early 2012 became the next target, with an official release and launch planned to coincide with the 70.3 Half Ironman event in May. If you are reading this book around this time, then I have succeeded. And if you are enjoying it enough, you can buy a couple of copies ready to give as Christmas presents at the end of the year if you like! Even though I became frustrated with each delay and not making the progress as fast as I was wanting, I am confident that the wait was worthwhile and the finished product was never too far away and being improved upon in the process. Most of the other goals I have, I will keep to myself for now, but a few have been shared with some people.

In order to reach my goals, my attitude is what I will have to work on the most. I am really trying to focus on keeping this positive, but it is definitely not easy. I know I will need a better attitude a lot more often, if I am to reach my dreams and goals for the years ahead. If I was to only reach half of them, I will still be happy, but that would be remaining average. I want to be above average in more of the things I do, and I hope I can inspire others to be as well. Whether or not I can win the constant battle against myself to become above average, I guess we'll all have to wait and see.

The following is a quote from a terrific New Zealand movie, starring Anthony Hopkins, which is definitely worth a look:

*If you don't follow through on your dreams, you might as well be a vegetable, a cabbage.*
**Burt Munro - The World's Fastest Indian**

## 26

# 3 Years On

*Success is connected with action. Successful people keep moving.*
*They make mistakes, but they don't quit.*
**Conrad Hilton**

On Wednesday 05 October 2011, I made enquiries with Royal Perth Hospital, as to when my upcoming knee operation might be. I was on the Orthopaedic waiting list scheduled for around November, but wanted to find out an approximate date as soon as possible, to organise work and make sure it didn't clash with any other events coming up. I was pleasantly surprised that there was a cancellation next week and my consultant Gavin Clarke was available to perform the operation then. I had almost become accepting of the fact that the current range of motion in my leg would be as much as I would ever have; as this was the first real chance that the Orthopaedic doctors had to try to make any real progress to improve the knee's flexion. I could either accept it and get on with life or go for improvement when the opportunity arose. I decided to go for improvement, so here's hoping it happens.

I debated long and hard about whether to add this chapter to my book. I wrote it as it happened, so that things were fresh in my mind and have only included it because it highlights the things that occurred during the week of the 3 year anniversary. The operation was scheduled for Tuesday morning, and as I prepared to leave Busselton, I couldn't help but be reminded that 3 years of Tuesdays ago, I was being flown to Royal Perth Hospital, shortly after my accident.

So, on Monday 10 October 2011, I was back at SPRC, the place I never wanted to return to. I had my preadmission appointments where I met my Anaesthetist and also my Resident Doctor, Gemma Smith. After going through what was required – and me telling them what would happen, because this whole scenario was such a familiar thing for me now – we discovered that when my surgery appointment was made, I wasn't actually booked into hospital until the day of the operation. This left me nowhere to stay in Perth, the night prior to surgery. Fortunately, a very organised and efficient nurse named Roanna was on duty, who got the wheels in motion, while I was having x-rays and blood tests done. I was soon booked into Well-Tel, the communal accommodation centre for out of town patients to stay at, who were having therapy or follow up sessions, but didn't require being admitted to hospital.

Between Roanna and Jane, the lovely fill-in coordinator from Well-Tel, I was all organised with a bed and given a meal voucher for the Shenton Park Café, the place I would escape to, as often as I could, last time I was at SPRC.

After an early dinner, it was off for a walk around the campus. This was a very weird and surreal feeling, walking through the corridors and hallways that I had only seen from a wheelchair. I saw a few familiar faces that I recognised, but had no idea of names or anything. I even made a cheeky walk into Ward 10, and poked my head into Room H, just to look. Everything in the Ward was exactly as I remembered it, including the bathroom, where I had so many showers lying on a trolley. I saw the main gymnasium and the smaller physiotherapy gym where I began my walking steps after weeks of lying down. Through the rabbit warren of corridors and pathways, I found a couple of the courtyards where Peta would take me to get some sun and fresh air when I was in the wheelchair. It was very strange to be back there and even stranger to be walking around.

The Well-Tel centre comprises nine bedrooms, four bathrooms, two kitchens, two living areas and feels more like staying in hotel than a hospital. Obviously they knew who I was, because I got the only room with its own ensuite! Very fortunate for me, once again! It was also strange being back in SPRC alone this time, with no support network around, but glad that I was fully independent and not relying on anyone to do things for me.

I was admitted to Ward 9 on this occasion and because I am classed as MRSA, it was my own room, yet again. Another win for me! I could not eat anything after 6:00 a.m. on Tuesday, so the rest of the morning was spent waiting to be taken through for surgery. Someone came in around 1:00 p.m. and drew a big arrow on my left leg, pointing up to my knee - just in case they weren't sure which one to operate on! My knee and the surrounding area was then shaven. After a series of swabs to see how contagious I was, I was left alone to relax. Finally, around 3:30 p.m. I was taken through. I never saw my Consultant, Gavin Clark, but I'm guessing he was in the operating room when the surgery occurred. The various checks were done and then I was given the magic gas and it was good night nurse, once again. Operation number 12 was here.

I was very confident of this surgery and excited to think that with this result, my leg would have massive, instant improvement and my mobility would be even better than it was currently. Thoughts of insignificant or even maybe worse results did begin to enter my mind, but I tried to remain positive and excited, almost wishing that after this operation, everything would be easier – cycling, running and the other daily tasks I found difficult or frustrating during recent times. This operation had to bring physical improvement, surely!

I recall asking the nurse for the time and hearing the reply that it was about 7:50 p.m. I think I had been back in my own room for around an hour, but I really have no firm idea. I was starving and was given a sandwich to eat, along with some Panadol, but I wasn't in much pain to worry about them. I was too drugged up still. My throat however was killing me and they must have been very rough putting the tubes inside me, as this was sore for days afterward and I was still coughing up blood 24 hours later. I slept for the rest of the evening, waking only to ask for more food or for the nurse to check my bladder. I was required to pee, but after not being able to drink since 5:00 a.m. I didn't really have much to let go, well over

12 hours later. Then came the threat of a catheter! A scan revealed what I knew all along, so I drank copious amount of water to fill myself up and provide the urine to get the nurse off my back, so I could then go back to sleep. It was so regimented for me to pee on demand, but being MRSA and a potential risk to other patients meant nothing, as very few staff members used gowns or gloves or masks when they came into my room. Yet another confusing frustration of the public health system!

After the operation, I had no feeling in my left leg above my knee. I could feel everything below it, including my toes, ankle and calf, but nothing else. It was a very strange feeling. I couldn't lift my leg or even feel the muscles to try and test the knee bend. It was like my upper leg was not part of me, but somehow the rest of it was.

The next morning, at around 7:45 a.m. my Registrar, Dr Taheri and my Resident, Dr Gemma Smith came in to see me and tell me what had happened. During the operation, they had scraped away the scar tissue from around my knee and the build-up below my kneecap, which was causing the most pain and restriction when bending. They were pleased with how the arthroscopy operation went and advised me that my knee bends quite well when I'm knocked out and unable to feel anything and they were able to get it nearly fully bent…shame it's not like that when I'm awake - yet! Isn't there a saying about having to move backwards in order to move forward, or something along those lines?

So now I just had to wait until the physiotherapist came through to give me the all clear about what I could do. Once I satisfied her that I could walk around the room without falling over, I was on the home straight. The nurse assigned to me, Annabel then brought in a trainee nurse to change my dressing and remove the cannula from my arm and get me sorted to go home. Some fun and games with these two, pretending that my leg hurt a lot more than it did kept the trainee on her toes, paranoid that she had hurt me, which gave Annabel and I plenty to laugh about. Finally, Dr Smith returned to give me the all clear and I was allowed to leave.

## 3 Years On

Once back in Busselton, it was a return to work on Thursday and my first physiotherapy session on Friday 14 October 2011. Today was the 3 year anniversary of my accident. I thought these things were meant to be happy occasions, but acknowledging an accident date is still worthy I suppose. After the week I was having, I really didn't know. I was having mixed emotions throughout the week, as things unfolded during this time, some of which had me wishing the whole week hadn't happened – much like the one around the same time, three years ago. I had made a very sizable mistake at work, prior to going to Perth and having to deal with the consequences of what happened as a result, was adding to my rollercoaster week of positives and negatives.

With Jeff already booked with another patient, I got the new physiotherapist, Gemma Harris, whose first innocent question was 'What have you done to yourself?' This just produced mass laughter from Jeff and me as we walked through to the treatment room. 'How long have you got?' was my response.

A very painful, but productive session with Gemma was the beginning of another long season of physiotherapy, as I made appointments for the next few weeks for further treatment. I guess Jeff and I will be entertaining each other for a while longer yet. All going well, I would be back cycling on Thursday and continuing on with my quest for a knee that bends more than 120 degrees.

As I left the physiotherapy practice, a wave of emotions came over me all at once and I was soon sitting in the car bawling my eyes out, over the week I had, culminating on the day's date. A successful knee operation which showed positive signs that I would gain a much bigger range of motion in the coming months was counteracted by the drama I had caused for myself at work, the results of which had serious implications for the business and me personally. Getting back into the routine of physiotherapy and the frustration that brings, as well as the unknown factors of results and time frames required to achieve them. The final turn of my rollercoaster week, was pathetically silly, in that I was worried that I had not made any major contributions to my book project for 3 – 4 days. I felt that I had lost my momentum and things were falling apart. I needed to get things back on track to keep up the progress we had made so far, which ironically led to the addition of this latest chapter. Very, very, silly!

Physiotherapy sessions continued and I would arrive early and do some exercises by myself on the stationary bike and the various stretching and strengthening machines in the practice. This next season of physiotherapy had to be more aggressive, so I was trying to get the muscles warmed up as much as I could, before Jeff took over. Then he would try and bend my knee as much as the pain would allow me to tolerate. I had actually lost bend since the operation and was back to around 100-115 degrees.

The sessions really, really hurt and I was even wondering if I was damaging other parts of my leg in order to gain improvement with my knee. My whole leg would ache for hours after I had finished with Jeff and it felt like I had gone back in time to early 2009 when we first started. The well-worn cliché 'No pain, no gain' was very appropriate once again and I really hoped that Jeff and I weren't going to have to put up with each other for another year, like last time, even though we did spend a great deal of time laughing and telling stories.

I would be lying if I said that I wasn't frustrated with the immediate results of the latest surgery. Facing another season of physiotherapy and redoing all of the same exercises and stretches to get my initial progress back before carrying on to even more flexion did not excite me at all. And the pain of forcing my knee to bend was not fun either. I expected and I wanted a faster, easier result this time. A big part of me felt that I deserved this; that I had earned it even, after spending the last 3 years doing as much as I could to get the results I wanted. It was like I was owed an instant result because I had gone through the struggle of slowly working away patiently beforehand.

But of course it doesn't work that way. I was reminded that by having it too easy, I wouldn't learn anything further or appreciate what I had when the good results came along. I tried riding my bike, over the next 2 weeks, but did not have enough flexion yet. I had success on the stationary bike, but only because I could adjust the seat easily and wasn't actually going anywhere.

Physiotherapy sessions twice a week continued and soon we were back to where we were before the last operation. The two main exercises that Jeff did were pushing my bent knee back and forth, trying to bring my heel in towards my torso while I was sitting on the therapy bench; and doing the same motion, but with me lying down on my stomach, while he brought my heel up towards my bottom. Both ways, had my knee bending to its maximum as Jeff slowly pushed it back and forth in small increments. I just had to lie there and suck up the pain as I could feel the progress he was making, but the pain brought me close to tears on several occasions. Soon I had enough bend to ride and by doing this regularly, it would help support the work that Jeff was doing.

Around mid-November, roughly a month after the operation, we had just over 120 degrees of bend and Jeff and I were both very pleased and surprised at how much this improvement made. We were both excited that there should be more to come and I was the most confident that I have ever been, that a larger range of motion would eventuate, over the next few months. I may not have 100% success, but I will be a lot happier with whatever I am given.

As the physiotherapy sessions continued, so the days passed in the lead up to IMWA on 04 December 2011. I had been coaching Aidan and Llando throughout the second half of the year and their moment of truth finally arrived as they dived in and headed out around the Busselton Jetty.

In his early thirties and in excellent physical condition, Llando showed a massive improvement in his swimming to surprise himself at how fast he made it back to shore. His ride began strong, but the rigors of the 180 km bike leg soon began to take its toll as he did his best to battle fatigue and the weather conditions during his first triathlon of any distance. As it is for most people, the run

## A Long Ride Back

is pure survival, so with plenty of time up his sleeve, he made the most of the excitement that comes with your first Ironman race, by mixing his running and walking with plenty of nutrition and hydration, as he cruised home well under fifteen hours. A superb result for him and his Coach!

A broken thumb, after a bike crash in mid-October, put a serious dent in Aidan's training for IMWA. Unable to swim, ride or run for 6 weeks and his hand in a cast, there was not a lot Aidan could do, but wait for the time to pass and then do the best he could on the day. As a self-confessed non-swimmer, Aidan made the most of his first journey around the jetty, taking nearly every possible second of the time allowed. His steady cycling had him back on track for the finish, but it would all come down to the run leg. With his energy levels heavily consumed by the swirling winds and rising temperatures, there was far too much walking going on, as far as his Coach was concerned. Some tough love was required, as he was 'encouraged' to run and walk between the various markers along the route. With time slipping away, the end of his fourth lap finally arrived, with the receipt of an orange armband to signify that he was allowed to enter the finish chute. As the race commentators built the crowd up, Aidan pulled out the sprint finish of his life to arrive on the line with less than 5 minutes to spare, after starting out nearly 17 hours earlier. It wasn't always pretty, but the job got done nonetheless, proving that a finish is a finish, regardless of the time!

As the 2011 race was unfolding, with me once again on the sidelines spectating and volunteering, the feelings of wanting to be out there again grew even more. I had been living vicariously through my friends training and race day, with all of the highs and lows that went along with them. The decision on whether or not to enter a future IMWA event would have to be made one day, but thankfully, not straight away.

So as 2011 came to an end, and 2012 began, I had a book that was nearly finished, a knee that was giving me a lot less grief than it used to; a 100% Ironman coaching success rate and a couple of

## 3 Years On

other projects to work on, which means that things are looking good for the near future! Busy, but good!

> *To succeed, you need something to hold on to, something to motivate you, something to inspire you.*
> **Tony Dorsett**

# 27

# It's All About You!

*No matter our age, nor our condition, there are still untapped possibilities within us and new beauty waiting to be born.*
**Dr Dale Turner**

So that's my story nearly done. Now let's talk about you. After all of this rambling on about me and my life, here is the challenge that I want to put out to you:

Think about what you want to do / have / change or accomplish. Then do something every day to work on achieving it. It might be simply reading more, making a phone call to someone you are hesitant to ring; listening to inspiring words or reading material more positive than what you are currently doing; or getting out and seeing, touching or researching what you want to have. Better still, find someone who has what you want and talk to them about how they got it. If you want to change jobs, start applying for a new one. If you want to do an Ironman, get a program and a Coach and start training. If you want to go for a holiday, pick a date and start saving. Nothing ever happens without a goal. This theory and talking about it, is the simple bit. The action is the hard part. Many things are simple, they just aren't easy.

And if your friends and family share their wisdom with you, which is always well meaning, and often has your best intentions at heart, but probably won't help you get what you want, simply remember that opinions are like belly buttons – everyone has one, but they aren't very useful!

Associating with positive people is very important to me, but the reality is that not all of my friends are positive all of the time. I wasn't positive all the time, so it made sense that they weren't and I couldn't expect them to be. One thing I learned very early on in my recovery was that there is always someone worse off than me. SPRC opened my eyes to a lot of people who were in a much worse condition physically than me and with other people around me, either friends or new acquaintances; they didn't necessarily have to be physically ill to be worse off either.

Some might be in a financial situation, or in a relationship that they are not happy with. A lot of people are stuck in an employment position and are miserable, but are too scared or too stuck in their comfort zone to do anything about it. Even just being open to looking at other opportunities that come along are often bypassed because their own thinking and the way their life is currently unfolding prevents them from making changes they know they need, but won't pursue or even consider. Many people are doing the same thing day after day, living a life of quiet desperation as they try to convince themselves that things are not that bad, while they wish for them to get better, somehow. Naturally, the same can also be said for relationships. Some people either don't want to be alone and stay together because they are more comfortable than anything else. Others need to decide whether they want to work on improving what they have and some need the courage to end the relationship altogether. The last few years seem to have had all of the above crashing through the surface for me.

Now, I am not claiming to have suddenly become an expert or some wannabe motivational speaker with all the answers, so please don't think that. I want my story to help motivate you to achieve your dreams and goals, just as I will need help and motivation to achieve my dreams and goals.

Some of the books that I read, or the movies I would watch for inspiration or to keep myself positive and try to break myself out of the negativity rut that I get in, are:

It's All About You!

## BOOKS

A Kick in the Attitude - *Sam Glenn*
Beyond Positive Thinking - *Arnold Fox, M.D. & Barry Fox, Ph.D.*
Change It! - *Dr. Bill Quain and Doug Price*
Eat That Frog! - *Brian Tracy*
Empower Yourself - *Clive Murphy*
Flight Plan - *Brian Tracy*
Go Girl! - *Olympic Gold Medallist Natalie Wood*
How To Win Friends And Influence People - *Dale Carnegie*
I'm Here To Win - *Chris McCormack*
It's Not About The Bike - *Lance Armstrong*
Lionheart - *Jesse Martin*
Never Tell Me Never - *Janine Sheppard*
Peaks & Valleys - *Spencer Johnson, M.D.*
Personality Plus - *Florence Littauer*
Put Your Dreams To The Test - *John Maxwell*
Scar Tissue - *Anthony Kiedis from the Red Hot Chili Peppers*
The Magic of Thinking Big - *David J Schwartz, Ph.D.*
The Secret - *Rhonda Byrne*
The Why Are You Here Café - *John P Strelecky*
Walking to Victory - *Adam Gilchrist*
Yes! - *John Fuhrman*
Yes Man - *Danny Wallace*
Your Dreams Are Too Small - *Joe Tye*

## MOVIES

Coach Carter
Invictus
Pay It Forward
Remember The Titans
The Pursuit of Happyness

The World's Fastest Indian
Varsity Blues
We Are Marshall

Many of these have been read or watched more than once over the past few years. Some were recommended, while others were found by chance. I can however, highly recommend all of them.

I am hoping you have noticed the quotes at the beginning and end of each chapter. These are just a portion of those that I have read or heard from various people over the years. I do not know the originality of some of them and have done my best to ensure that the correct people are credited, so I won't get sued! They don't all relate to me and my story necessarily, but I believe they are all worthy of inclusion, some of which I have done simply because I liked them. You may need to read them a couple of times, for them to sink in.

So I hope my journey through this book inspires you to set some goals and achieve them in your own life, regardless of your age, sex, physical ability, perceived intelligence, or the current position of where you are today. I don't think there is anything special about me, but I have managed to achieve a few things that are quite cool. HIM and Ironman finishes; surviving a serious bike accident and the return to cycling and the sport of triathlon; coaching junior athletes and passing on my skills, knowledge and enthusiasm for a sport which interests them; and writing a book are just some of them. You may think these achievements are pretty good – you may not. As I said at the beginning of this book, I wasn't necessarily very good at doing what I did; I just didn't give up on everything when times got tough. I know that 'the glass is half full attitude' can be a well-worn cliché, but dwelling on the negative is just not very much fun! So if you have related a little bit to my story, then I wish you all the best and if I can help in anyway, don't be shy!

It's All About You!

*The most important thing in life is to stop saying 'I wish' and start saying 'I will'. Consider nothing impossible, then start treating possibilities as probabilities.*
***David Copperfield***

# 28

# Dear Diary...

*The future belongs to those who believe
in the beauty of their dreams.*
***Eleanor Roosevelt***

The book we used for a diary over the 3 months I was in hospital was another way of keeping positive, through all the support I was getting from the people around me. Most entries were from those who visited and their standard 'get well soon' messages. The best thing about this was that everyone could write their own words in it and also see what others had written too. This was of course, when I was coherent enough to give it to them!

The diary was a great idea, but I wish I had shared it with my visitors more often. There were times that I myself even forgot the book was there and some people never even knew it existed. Luckily most came back a second time and were able to write notes and well wishes in it for me then. Ross came to RPH a number of times, but didn't find out about the book until I was at Shenton Park, weeks later! He was not impressed! Important information for me was what gifts and flowers came from different people and organisations; phone messages and visitors who came to see me when I was off having surgery or x-rays; or passed out like a drug addict!

I highly recommend that if anyone you know has to go to hospital and it looks like they will be there for a while, then use a book or diary to record events and progress. Details, memories and well-wishes from friends and family can definitely help with the recovery and healing process and are a terrific reminder to look back on in future years.

Just a few of the messages from the visitors who wrote words of encouragement are:

There's no Tuff'n'Up left in Busselton! *Max, Jenny & Belinda Higgins*

Go Forward Young Man! *Cameron Williams*

Didn't bring any flowers, just incredible company! *Mike Taylor*

Came to say gidday and was disgusted that there was a waiting line for a chair. Great to see you looking well though. *Jeff Coventry*

Came to carry out my weekly list of tasks. *Purds*

Tough times don't last…but tough people do. Kick it in the arse, Shaggy. *Russell Vitale*

Steve looks wonderful compared to what I expected. *Leonie Paine*

So good to see you. The light at the end of the tunnel is now bigger. When you come home I will charge you for those foot massages. *Sharon Nisbet*

Came to see you. You were preparing for surgery and resting. But still looking very hot! *Donna Chatfield*

Got the All Blacks shirt on, watching New Zealand v Ireland. (beer and popcorn missing) *Jo Wilson*

Next weekend we will do the breakout. Don't take 'no' for an answer. *Ross Pedlow*

Came back from Bali, especially to see you. *Tamlyn Dillon*

Steve, your toes on the right foot looked rooted! *Andy Milne*

Good to see you've still got a sense of humour mate. No doubt you will be back on the bike in no time. We are all thinking of you back in Busselton. *Deon Homer*

Welcome home Alli! Let's move all Steve's stuff. *Allison Slack*

## Dear Diary...

Kia Kaha and Go Hard. All the best from team 'Aotearoa'. *Jason Hapeta*

Busso people are strong, be it...challenges like this are there to test us... *Ross Pedlow*

Came to visit and bought water and cake! *Susan Arthur*

You are...amazing...so vibrant, so positive...so strong. You are going to get through this...you have so many friends that are with you 100%. *Peta McAuliffe*

8:00 p.m. and it's good night nurse! *Jo Wilson*

Alli came to visit. Drove Alex up, went shopping, brought Macca's and took photos of you sitting up in the chair. Yaaa! Anything else, just call. *Allison Slack*

Here with Steve, the poor cripple. Living the life of luxury – In bed with choices, laptop & TV. With meals provided – what more could anyone wish for! Live it up Steve, you'll be back to the hectic life all too soon. *Judy Rustean*

Sorry for taking so long, but we have been thinking of you every day. You are motivation & inspiration to us all. *Louise Leyden*

Awesome to see you out on the course and had a tear in my eye as I watched you almost launch yourself out of the wheelchair. *Connie Watson*

Looking great Shaggy, your progression is very impressive and a credit to all your strength and hard work. *Tineke Hancey*

Finally got here. Not that you are far from our thoughts always. Needless to say you have your own private Physios waiting to get their hands on you when you return. *Katie Greenfield*

Massive improvement in you Steve, keep up the good work. *Julie Bray*

# A Long Ride Back

Looking good. Skinny, but good! ***Rob & Glenis Slack***

Life is good, but not as you know it. Head down, butt up and move forward. You're definitely heading the right way. Well done. ***Alex Douglas***

You big girl! ***Belinda Higgins***

We miss your smiley face. Thinking of you often. ***Wendy Paine***

Looks like you were having a good sleep, so I didn't wake you. They wouldn't even let me in, so I tiptoed my way through and found you. ***Lajos Varga***

Keep up the speedy recovery and look forward to having a beer with you very soon. ***Michael Bray***

*Most notable winners encountered heartbreaking
obstacles before they triumphed.
They win because they refused to become
discouraged by their defeats.*
B. C. Forbes

## 29

# Thanking The Cool Kids!

*There is no limit to what can be accomplished,
if it doesn't matter who gets the credit.*
**Ralph Waldo Emerson**

Where do I begin? This list is not in any order and barely even touches the surface of those who have helped me with my recovery since the day of my accident.

So I'll say a massive Thank You to everyone who visited; brought me chocolate; phoned; emailed; brought in food and snacks; lent me movies to watch; brought in more chocolate and kept me updated on what was happening in the outside world as you helped me eat the chocolate. Those who prayed; brought me books, magazines, games and more chocolate; and ran around after me, getting the things I needed. Others who brought me gifts, flowers and cards; and still more chocolate; who picked me up and dropped me off when I needed to get into town, listened to me talk rubbish and put up with me rambling on in my drugged up stupors! Your support meant a lot then and it still does now.

I hope that reading my book might help people to understand what life is like from a patient's perspective and some of the things that go on inside their head. I also hope that I can be as caring and supportive to others who may need it from me one day.

Thank you to all of the medical staff who assisted me from the day of the crash, right through my hospital stays. From the St Johns Ambulance personnel and Busselton Hospital staff, through to the Royal Flying Doctors Service who got me to Perth. The emergency team, Intensive Care Unit and Major Trauma Ward staff at Royal

Perth Hospital through to everybody at Shenton Park Rehabilitation Campus. This extends to my Case Manager, Sheryl Jonescu; Dr Anthony Williams, Plastic Surgeon; along with Dr Wyson Wong, who I seemed to see nearly every day I was in hospital, throughout all of my visits to RPH. Dr Gavin Clark, Orthopaedic Surgeon, right through the chains of command, Registrars, Doctors, Nurses, Orderlies, Cleaners and Service Staff. Everyone has an important role to play in the daily running of the hospital and I thank you all for the jobs that you do. The nurses in particular are highly under-rated as far as I am concerned, as they are the ones who are with the patients all day and all night and have to put up with far more than their pay cheque would probably cover.

Peta McAuliffe, Allison Slack, Rosemary 'Purds' Goldsmith and Aidan Midgley were all incredibly supportive and arranged anything I needed whether in hospital or at home. I will always be in debt to you four wonderful people. Thank you again for everything you did.

Fabio, Mickey B, Mr Busselton and The Red Rocket. Sorry for the really bad ending to a really great ride. I've managed to get out with some of you boys a few times since being back on the bike, and I plan on being out there for many more to come.

Most of my friends did things for me that I never knew about and probably don't have to know about, simply because that's what friends do. You will know more than me what you did and I thank you for that. I hope that by reading my story, you realise how appreciative I am of this and that you gain some understanding of what life was like from where I was standing (or lying). Being the recipient of this love and attention was very gratifying and made me feel very special.

*It's not where you start, it's where you finish.*
**Gillian Hennessy-Ortega**

# 30

# The Fab Four And Other Rock Stars

*A great pleasure in life is doing what people say you cannot do.*
*Walter Gagehot*

I talk about a lot of people in my book, and so I think it is appropriate to share with everyone, a little bit about those who have played a significant role in my life, over the past few years.

Max Higgins is Mr Busselton. There are a few impersonators in town, but this man is the real deal. As the only local competitor in the first IMWA in 2004, Max has been there ever since, along with three trips to Port Macquarie to keep Michael company. With his lovely wife Jenny, often by his side on race day, Max inspires many of the Busselton triathletes with his experience and durability to keep racing year after year. Max's laid back and relaxed attitude always sees him calm and composed for every race, confident that his training will get him through whatever the race dishes out. Max has turned many heads when he removes his shirt to reveal a physique that many men half his age would envy. Christmas at the Higgins house in 2007 has been a highlight of my life and I enjoy spending time with Max, Jenny and Belinda either out on the road, or relaxing on their balcony, watching the sun set over Geographe Bay.

Michael Bray is Invincible! After having a heart attack in his late thirties, he found the sport of cycling and was instantly drawn to triathlon. A number of years as President of the Busselton Swimming Club have seen him Coach plenty of talented juniors, including his own sons, Ben and Louis. A horrible crash in 2007 involving four other bikes and a kangaroo saw him break a couple of vertebrae in his neck. He has gone on to make a full recovery with a career that boasts six IMWA finishes and five IMOZ finishes in Port

## A Long Ride Back

Macquarie. Later this year, he is heading to America for Ironman St George, in Utah as he keeps his record of two Ironman races every year, for the past 5 years. Michael has been well and truly bitten by the triathlon bug, adding six Busselton HIM finishes as well as one in the Gold Coast. After a successful year in 2011, he will again be coaching his squad of Tuff-n-Up Iron-virgins and repeat offenders across the line at Busselton's HIM and IMWA this year. His wife Julie is also an IMWA finisher and further testament that whatever you throw at the Bray family, they will fight it, defeat it and send it packing!

I met Alex Douglas in 2006, when he came over from Scotland to compete in IMWA. We got on really well and he quickly became an honorary Busselton local, joining us for our training sessions and earning himself the title of 'The Red Rocket'. It was great to see him return for the 2008 event and bringing his wife, Marie and daughter, Madison over for a holiday, meant that they could see why he loved returning and how terrific the people of Busselton are. I firmly believe that the Ironman was secondary to why Alex was over here that year. He was riding with me that day for a reason and although none of us would have known that then, there are many people who are glad that his cool head was with us that day.

Steve 'Fabio' Anstee has been doing triathlons since he was a kid. A few years out of the sport, saw him return with all of the natural talent he has always possessed. Steve accomplished a childhood dream of his to compete at the Ironman World Championships in Hawaii, after he qualified at IMWA in December 2010. The Busselton locals watched with bated breath in October 2011, as he took to the stage in Kona demonstrating once again that pain is just weakness, leaving his body! Steve has an infectious personality and has plenty of male fans as well as his endless following of ladies. He keeps you honest when he's training with you and knows how to hurt himself in the process, which usually occurs once he has finished hurting you. Another serial offender when it comes to crashing bikes, his effort in February 2012 bought back nasty memories and I am relieved that he made it through in one piece.

## The Fab Four And Other Rock Stars

There aren't many other guys I would have wanted with me on Tuesday 14 October 2008. I'm sure the fab four would have traded places with anyone that day, but I for one wouldn't have given them up for anything. Thanks again lads, I owe you one!

I met Rosemary Purdie as she was known then, when Aidan and I interviewed her for a job in the Accounts Department at The Geographe Bayview Resort, in early 2005. Aidan and I had known her partner Brad Goldsmith, through cycling in Busselton, but hadn't realised they were together until after we employed her. Purds, as she is known to most people, would provide endless entertainment at work and her ability with accounting and organising our office made me look great! Getting to know Brad and Purds has given me the privilege of attending their wedding and I have watched both their sets of boys grow from skinny little kids, to towering teenagers and local soccer stars. Brad and Purds are one of the best couples I know and are a testament to the fact that if things don't work out the first time around, meeting the partner of your dreams may only be one CPR lesson away!

Peta McAuliffe and I had known each other for a few years before my accident and got together after I began helping her with some running training she was doing. Our friendship grew into a relationship, which unfortunately was ruined several months after the accident. I can't thank Peta enough for all the love and support she showed me during that time and I am glad that we have become friends again since. Her positive attitude and focused determination has seen her cross the Ironman finishing line as well, even when she wondering what on earth she was doing, on more than one occasion.

Aidan Midgley has been my boss, on and off since 1993 in New Zealand and was the one who invited me over to work in Busselton towards the end of 2000 and I haven't moved back yet. Over the years since I have been living in Busselton, Aidan has become very much like my second dad. He's the guy I go to for advice, help or other problems, or just to hang out with. We started riding together back in 2005, took swimming lessons together and have participated in an Ironman in a team. Aidan was one of the main instigators and supporters of me doing my first Ironman, back in 2006. After my accident, Aidan would be up to visit as often as his job allowed and would bring anything I needed, whether it was a pie for lunch or a recording of an All Blacks rugby match for us to watch. When he wasn't visiting, he was taking care of the things that I couldn't, which included getting the necessary paperwork for my various insurances; and making the phone calls to deal with the claims agents; getting things happening; so that the process began sooner, rather than later.

One of Aidan's favourite movies is The Transporter, starring Jason Statham. His character, Frank, transports objects anywhere, no questions asked, for a fee of course and his number one rule is 'Don't change the plan'. So, whenever I needed something delivered, I called Aidan – The Transporter! The remarkable thing about all of the visits Aidan made was that he absolutely hates hospitals and any sign of a needle, or medical talk would have him looking for the door. Luckily for me, he really went outside his comfort zone to hang out and stay as long as he did. In fact, for most people visiting me, who was so out-of-it on medication, it must have been pretty boring and definitely not much fun. Aidan was one of the confidants I went to when thoughts about printing this book became serious and his opinion and ideas have all been invaluable. His plan was to do an Ironman before he turned 60, so 2011 was the year he chose. It was satisfaction, relief, pride and lots of emotion, all rolled into one, as he ran down the finishing chute and crossed the finish line, even with a couple of minutes to spare, after a very long day at the office. But as we say in the sport of Ironman - a finish is a finish! Sunday 04 December 2011, is the day he joined the Ironman family.

Allison Slack worked with us at the resort in Busselton and moved in with me, when she needed a place to live in 2007. Although I haven't got her on a proper bike yet, she loves watching the big triathlons and has even been converted to soccer, scoring her first career goal in 2011, a wonderful Mother's Day present for Glenis to witness. Allison spent many hours running around after me when I finally got home and was always making sure I wasn't doing too much or getting too risky, as my confidence grew. One of the positives to come out my accident was Allison's introduction to my friends within the cycling and triathlon community who welcomed her in with open arms and I am privileged to be the one who brought her warmth and love into their lives as well.

Allison's parents Rob and Glenis welcomed me into their extended family Christmas gathering in 2008 and made all of my problems disappear, if only for a very short time.

Allison works for Clive and Margaret Johnson, at Mandalay Holiday Park, who were also very understanding and flexible with allowing Allison time off work, particularly during the first few days after my accident. Thanks also have to go to Clive and Margaret for helping me get the majority of my story written, even though they were unaware that they had contributed in any way.

Jo Wilson was another regular Perth visitor often followed by her young grandson Dylan whose innocence when asking blunt questions kept us entertained as well. Most of Jo's visits began with bringing me in hot chocolate and other tasty snacks as an alternative to the repetitive hospital food. Again, anything I needed was only a phone call away and Jo did her best to keep my diary up to date and accurate every time she was there.

Andy Milne is the one responsible for getting me back on a bike. The ultimate wingman for any new, inexperienced rider or rehabilitated nervous wreck, who needs a lot of confidence rebuilt. I could sook all I wanted to Andy, but he wasn't having any of it. It was an honour being the MC at his wedding to Robyn in 2009, who has brought with her plenty of reasons for Andy to get out of bed each day as well as reasons to stay in bed sometimes too. Their delightful daughter Madison adds to their happiness together and we all look forward to the day when she stops bursting into tears, whenever she sees me!

Connie Watson has led the charge of Busselton locals who refused to give up when things got tough. An inspiration to many people after surviving the Bali Bombings in 2002, I am honoured to have her name next to mine on the Paul Goodwin memorial trophy of the Busselton Half Ironman event. Her counselling and friendly chats over coffee helped me to get back out there doing things, when I was too scared and embarrassed of the way my body has been changed. Not even a broken toe, 2 weeks before IMWA in 2011 was going to stop her from reaching the starting line that year, demonstrating once again how determined and mentally strong this amazing lady is.

Ross Pedlow will always be my Coach, regardless of whether I am Ironman training or not! He agreed to take me on board back in 2007, when he didn't have to, but obviously saw how passionate and keen I was at that time. Getting me down to Busselton for IMWA was simply amazing and I can't thank him enough for helping me with this goal! Thank you so much for writing the foreword for my book and for all the faith and support you have shown me over the years. I look forward to continuing our successful partnership in the near future.

Jeff and Katie Greenfield from Physio SouthWest made me an offer I simply could not refuse and was probably not allowed to refuse. Your time, energy and patience in helping me achieve my 2010 and 2011 HIM finishes were something I will never be able to repay you for. Words cannot express how grateful I am to you both for what you have done for me and what you continue to do for me. If I never have to have Jeff's elbow anywhere near my groin ever again, I will be very happy, but I think we all know that that is certain to happen again at some point. Katie qualifying for Hawaii at IMWA in 2011 was a tremendous reward for all of the hard work she does in training and we are thrilled that she will have a chance to shine on Kona's big stage.

Kym and Sharon Nisbet are another fabulous Busselton couple who have become very important to me over the past few years. From our mutual passion for cycling, to employing me in their business and adopting me as yet another one of the many sons they have inherited, I have always been made to feel welcome in their home and they have offered to help me in any way they can, regardless of the situation. Kym and Sharon's strength of character has been tested far too often in recent years, but their commitment and determination to keep fighting has seen them overcome all of the challenges they have faced. Their son Joel is a constant source of encouragement to both of them, with his attitude to live life to the full every day. Kym inspired many of us himself with his return to cycling after a serious illness and Sharon continues to display the strength she often doesn't realise she has, proving that no challenge is too great for the wonderful and unbeatable Mrs Nisbet.

Over the past few seasons of coaching, I have had the fortunate pleasure of inflicting a lot of pain, on a very talented up and coming triathlete, Josh Rabjones. Towards the end of November 2011, I set a goal for Josh, which was to ride for 100 days in a row, either on the road or the wind trainer, for a minimum of half an hour, so that he would have the option of very easy days, when he got tired and to allow for all the other activities he does, especially when school returned. Initially Josh was very apprehensive, as it meant riding from the end of November, through until the beginning of March. The purpose of the challenge was to ultimately improve his riding, but also to build on his self-belief. As the days went on, the improvement was almost instant and as the weeks progressed, Josh became more determined to complete the challenge. I thought it was only fair that as his Coach, I should be subject to the same conditions. I am more than confident that by the time you read this, we will have completed the task and reached day 100, thanks largely to the support that we have been getting from the people around us. Coaching Josh and spending time with new triathletes who are just getting involved in the sport, has given me added excitement and it is great living vicariously through their training and events, while seeing the pleasure on their faces when they cross the finish line. I never had the natural talent that Josh does, but watching his naive excitement as he realises how much he can push himself adds to my passion for helping him improve. Josh has a big future ahead of him and I believe he can go a long way in this sport, because he definitely has the determination to do it. Josh's focus and commitment to riding for 100 days in a row has kept me excited and disciplined as well, to make sure we both completed the challenge.

> *If one advances confidently in the direction of his dreams, and endeavours to live the life which he has imagined, he will meet with a success, unexpected in common hours.*
> **Henry David Thoreau**

# 31

# Further Acknowledgements

*Do not follow where the path may lead. Go instead
where there is no path and leave a trail.*
*Ralph Waldo Emerson*

When I first had the idea to write this book, it was nothing more than a distant wish. But as the pages grew and chapters were added, it became a dream. As I got closer to reaching the end, it became my goal and my passion. I had found the reason why I couldn't sleep at night and couldn't stay in bed in the mornings, even when it was still cold out. Many rides and other tasks were postponed because I wanted to get chapters finished or changes made as I strived to reach my self-imposed deadlines.

But after the realisation of how much this project would potentially cost, my dream began to waver and the doubts started to creep in as to whether I should even continue. I even began to doubt that my story was worth writing, or even reading, let alone worth buying. Once again though, the support of my close friends and associates encouraged me and gave me the ideas needed to persist and look at all possible options, regardless of what they might be or what I might have to do.

Making enquiries to seek the financial assistance I thought I was going to need was not something I felt comfortable doing, but was part of the journey and the learning experience I was going through along the way. I had 'finished' my book a number of times over the 8-10 months prior to getting it published. But as each person who read it, gave their honest and valued positive criticism, I began to discover that what I was trying to say and what I had written were often poles apart.

Seeking advice from a wide variety of people, from all different areas, helped give me options and led to finding out all that was required to get this project off the ground. Some paths led to good ideas and good people, while others led to dead ends. But as another great saying goes – if the dream is big enough, the facts don't count.

Purds told it to me straight with many parts of my story as we edited and reworked each chapter and spent countless hours writing until we were both happy with everything. This is as much her book as it is mine and I will always be in debt to her unconditional support. Hopefully we have done alright!

Leonie Paine worked her graphic design magic on the cover and the photos throughout my book, making sure the pictures were as professional as possible. Luckily for me, both of these ladies take payment in the form of wine, so once I waved a bottle in front of them, my requests were acted on immediately.

Thank you to everyone who supplied photos for me and held the camera when required over the years. I hope I have acknowledged everybody properly, so please accept my apologies if I have listed anybody incorrectly.

Roger Paine gets the credit for the funky little triathlete figurines at the end of each chapter. He understood what I wanted before I was even sure myself and fine-tuned his ideas to suit my descriptions.

Julie-Ann Harper from MBS Press answered all of my questions, regardless of how silly and trivial they were. Her commitment to ensuring my work achieved the best result was evident from the day we met and the self-publishing journey was a much smoother process with her assistance, than trying to do everything myself. Her professionalism in helping me tell my story showed through her dedication to making sure all of my concerns were taken care of as soon as they arose.

The following people and organisations have been instrumental

# Further Acknowledgements

in helping me fulfil the dream of publishing my book. Thank you for the assistance you have provided me.

| | |
|---|---|
| Aidan Midgley | Kellie Markwell |
| Allison Slack | Kym & Sharon Nisbet |
| Andy & Robyn Milne | Leonie Paine |
| Anthony & Tasha Pickersgill | Llando Pyke |
| Belinda Higgins | Marathon Photos |
| Brad & Rosemary Goldsmith | Margaret Purdie |
| Busselton Jetty Swim Cmte | Mitchell Anderson |
| Cate Finlay | Professor Fiona Wood |
| City of Busselton Council | Rick Keehan |
| Clive & Margaret Johnson | Rob & Glenis Slack |
| Connie Watson | Roger Paine |
| Connors Sports Management | Ross Pedlow |
| Fiona Docherty | Royal Flying Doctor Service |
| Jeff & Suzie Trott | Sue Schleuter |
| Jo Wilson | Trevor Fitzgerald |
| Julie-Ann Harper | Triathlon Western Australia |
| Kathy Atkinson | Wayne & Peta Pickersgill |

Portions of the proceeds from the sale of this book will be donated to the Royal Flying Doctor Service; the Cancer Society of New Zealand; and other local worthy causes.

Thank you for your support.

*Reaching your goal is about the <u>prize</u> you get,*
*not the <u>price</u> you pay.*
**Unknown**

## 32

# What Now?

*Do not wish to be anything but what you are,*
*and endeavour to be that perfectly.*
**St. Francis De Sales**

By the time I had finished writing this book, I was meant to have told an incredible story about returning to the sport of triathlon and finishing another Ironman Western Australia event, to share with everybody how I had completed my comeback to a sport which had brought me so many highs and lows over the years. I haven't done another Ironman yet, but by finishing two HIM events, I think I am close to achieving what I set out to do by telling my story. Some may agree some might not – but it's only their belly button talking, isn't it! People have told me that by simply getting onto a bike again is more than enough. Others have said that doing a triathlon of any distance is enough; while some people can't believe that I have done one HIM after what happened, let alone two.

Two halves definitely do not make a full, as far as Ironman events go, so once I am satisfied that I am ready for the challenge the next stage of the plan can begin. My leg is bending a lot better now and with a larger range of motion, I hope to be running and cycling even better than I have in the past few years, all going well.

I haven't made it back onto the soccer pitch yet either and I don't know whether I will. I've seen too many knee injuries from stronger, fitter and more skilful players that I doubt a damaged knee with a deficient Anterior Cruciate Ligament would have any chance with sidesteps; running on uneven surfaces and slide tackles. Best leave the running for straight lines I think! I'm not ruling it out and still love watching games as often as I can. When I do see my

# A Long Ride Back

friends out there playing, I still think 'maybe' or 'what if', but at the moment, it's not a priority. If the day does come though, there would have to be one condition - Brad Goldsmith has to be out there on the pitch with me!

As for the rest of the story, the part where I cross the finish line of IMWA and hear those four magical words, that send shivers down your spine and make you feel like you are the king of the world, will have to wait. The rigors of training for long distance triathlons; combining three sports together to become one, are about as much as my body has been able to handle in the last three years. I have too much respect for the Ironman, which is why the 2010 and 2011 events weren't pursued. 2012 has been on my mind for a while, but whether it eventuates, we will all have to wait and see.

I will do an Ironman again, but it needs to be on my terms, and no one else's. There is unfinished business out there on the course and even though the medals I have remind me that I am an Ironman, I need to hear the words shouted out to me one more time. Having Michael Bray and Connie Watson hang the finisher's medal around my neck would make this even better.

So until then, I guess the only thing left to say is - "I'll see you out there!"

To be continued…

www.ingramcontent.com/pod-product-compliance
Lightning Source LLC
Chambersburg PA
CBHW071229080526
44587CB00013BA/1545